Roger Zimmerman

Social Science PROJECTS YOU CAN DO

Social Science Science PROJECTS YOU CAN DO

by

Thomas P. Weinland and
Donald W. Protheroe

Illustrated by Ted Schroeder

PRENTICE-HALL, INC., ENGLEWOOD CLIFFS, N.J.

The letter in the chapter entitled *Advice* is from the book
ANN LANDERS TALKS TO TEENAGERS ABOUT SEX by Ann Landers
© 1963 by Prentice-Hall, Inc. Published by Prentice-Hall,
Inc., Englewood Cliffs, New Jersey.

Book design by Dana Kasarsky

Social Science Projects You Can Do
by Thomas P. Weinland and Donald W. Protheroe
Copyright © 1973 by Thomas P. Weinland and Donald W. Protheroe
Illustrations © 1973 by Prentice-Hall, Inc.

10   9   8   7   6   5   4   3   2

Printed in the United States of America • 2

Prentice-Hall International, Inc., London
Prentice-Hall of Australia, Pty. Ltd., North Sydney
Prentice-Hall of Canada, Ltd., Toronto
Prentice-Hall of India Private Ltd., New Delhi
Prentice-Hall of Japan, Inc., Tokyo

Library of Congress Cataloging in Publication Data

Weinland, Thomas P
      Social science projects you can do.
      1.   Social sciences—Juvenile literature.   2.   Social
sciences—Problems, exercises, etc.   I.   Protheroe,
Donald, joint author.   II.   Schroeder, Ted, illus.
III.   Title.
H95.W44   300'.7'2   72–8098
ISBN 0–13–818260–4

CONTENTS

SOCIAL SCIENCE PROJECTS YOU CAN DO

CONTENTS

To: Ricky, Chris and Jay
and
Don and Parrish

INTRODUCTION

The social sciences include such subjects as economics, sociology, anthropology, political science and geography. Sometimes history and psychology are also included in this group of subjects. Each of these subjects studies something about man and the way he lives. Economics, for example, is the study of the way human beings make a living; the way they make, trade and consume goods and services. Political science studies the way men govern themselves. Geography studies the way man lives in his physical environment. History studies all of these things as they occurred in the past.

These subjects have developed because humans are curious about themselves. They have asked such questions as:

1. In what ways are all humans alike?
2. In what ways are humans different? What makes them different?
3. What makes a good leader?
4. How should man spend a limited amount of money? 9
5. How does the past influence the present?

In order to answer these questions men began to study society, the environment, business, government and the past. From these studies have emerged the social sciences.

SOCIAL SCIENCE PROJECTS YOU CAN DO

To answer the questions man has about himself, social scientists conduct some form of research. Often the research involves counting things. The political scientist might count votes in districts with a high percentage of wealthy families to see if a candidate's appeal to the business vote had been successful. A sociologist might count the number of children in wealthy families and compare his studies with earlier ones to see if wealthy families today are smaller than those ten years ago. An anthropologist might count the number of children in wealthy families in Japan, India and in Kenya to see if the size of such families varies in different countries. An economist might count the ways in which wealthy families spent their money and compare this with the way poor people spent their money.

Research involves various forms of investigation. Anthropologists might study the way people use words. Historians might read diaries or examine pictures and cartoons of a certain year to learn what people were most interested in. A geographer might use a map to observe the influences of transportation routes—highway, railroad, airport and river—on the growth of a city.

As social scientists do all their research, they learn from each other. In investigating the problems of American cities, they find that each social science subject is related to other subjects. In the same way, the subject you know as social studies in school probably draws on all of the social science subjects. As you learn about a certain country or a certain period in history, you are also learning about areas of research of all social scientists.

This book has been written to give you a chance to be a social scientist. You can conduct research to learn more about yourself, your family and your community. In doing some of the projects in this book, you can learn a lot about how social scientists conduct research. Far more important, you can learn a lot about human beings, which, after all, is what social science and social studies are all about.

Asking questions is the key to any research. In the following projects we suggest questions or issues. We also suggest approaches for answering these questions. You can think of your own questions and your own approaches to the answers—they may very well be better than ours.

Once you set up a question and a way to answer it, you must then collect the information. You may have to count things or conduct interviews or read books and periodicals—perhaps all three. With the information collected you can begin to draw some conclusions. We must warn you that your conclusions probably will be limited. One of the greatest dangers in any research is making broad generalizations. If your information was gathered in your school, you can generalize only about *your school.* It is tempting to conclude that all schools are like yours. But don't bet on it! One of the things you will learn in research is that absolutely "right" answers aren't always right —there may be exceptions. Once you have "finished" your study, continue to keep your eyes and ears and mind open. Your answers may need to be changed.

Suggest your ideas to other students in your school and in other schools. If their conclusions are the same as yours, your answers can be more widely applied. You can also test your answers by reading. Other social scientists may have reached conclusions similar to yours. It is not important that your answers apply to all people and phenomena everywhere. If the experience you gained in finding your answers helps you to understand the world around you, your project and research have been worthwhile. We hope you enjoy the book. We hope you'll enjoy working with social science projects. Good luck.

REPORTING YOUR STUDY

Once you've asked a question and found some answers, you'll probably want to tell people about it. You may want to show your answers to the whole school or just talk your conclusions over with your family. You may want to take action by presenting your findings to an official body like your town council or local newspaper. In any case, by pulling your information together you can learn a great deal more about your project. New questions may come up. You may see a relationship between two entirely different studies you've conducted.

One obvious way to report your findings is to write a report —a description of the project, your procedures and your results. Here are some other methods you might use to display your research.

Charts

If you used a questionnaire in your project, you can set up a chart to illustrate your findings. Assuming you had five photographs of hair and beard styles and five statements that encouraged people to judge the attractiveness of each, your chart might look like this:

Picture Statement	Findings		
	Agree	Disagree	No Opinion
1 He should shave his beard.	30 (60%)	15 (30%)	5 (10%)
2 He should cut his hair shorter.			
3 He should trim his beard.			
4 He is very attractive.			
5 He is not attractive.			

Under "Agree," "Disagree" and "No Opinion" list the number and percentage of those who answered. At the bottom of your chart indicate how many people answered your questionnaire.

For the project on mobility you could set up a chart indicating how many families moved in and out of your town in each year that you checked.

	1870	1890	1910	1930	1950	1970
Moved into XYZ Junction	20	33	28	28	75	82
Moved out of XYZ Junction	19	17	21	18	38	42

SOCIAL SCIENCE PROJECTS YOU CAN DO

Graphs

Most of the information you put in chart form can also be placed on a graph. In the mobility project you could use a line graph like the one below. The horizontal line shows the years; the vertical line the number of people.

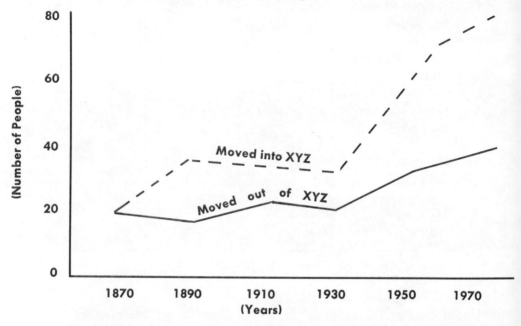

Use different colors or different types of lines (broken, straight, dots) to illustrate movement in and out of XYZ Junction.

A bar graph is better for comparing several things, whereas a line graph is better for illustrating trends over the years. You might use a bar graph for a time-study project.

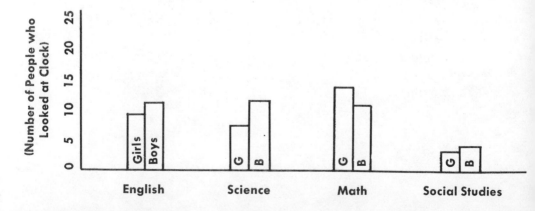

REPORTING YOUR STUDY

You can compare student clock watchers with rush-hour clock watchers, but the number of people observed must be the same for each group. If the class has 25 students, then be sure to watch 25 commuters (or shoppers) and observe both groups for the same length of time. If you have different numbers in each group, use percentages—10 clock watchers in 10 minutes in a 25-student class is 40%. Twenty clock watchers in 10 minutes for a group of 100 commuters is 20%. Graph it like this:

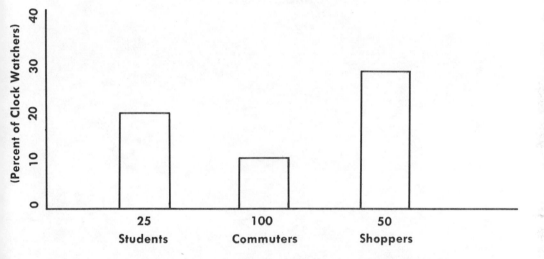

Use a circle graph to illustrate proportions. One example would be the project on how much money is spent for your needs. Assuming the total expenditure is $1000 a year and that your clothes cost $200 and food $400, it would look like this:

15

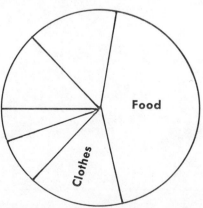

Maps

The projects relating to mobility and history can also be presented on a map. You can use colored pins or stars to show where in the United States your family has lived. Different colors can represent different generations. You can do the same with a world map to illustrate the countries from which your ancesters came.

The ideas here are meant to be suggestions. You can use all of these forms together, showing your information in several ways. You can also use pictures, tape recordings, cartoons and other materials to illustrate your point.

1

ADVICE

Dear Ann (Landers):

I'm a high school senior and I've laughed my head off at some of the troubles you've printed, but if you can help me I'll never laugh again.

My problem is my girl. She thinks the front seat of my car is a sofa and that I'm a chair. If she isn't almost on my lap, her arms are wrapped around my neck. She distracts me and sometimes blocks my vision. After a few close calls, I have pleaded with her to please let me drive the car with both hands. She says that four eyes are better than two and that she is always on the lookout.

If I have an accident I'll be grounded for life. My dad is strict about the car (it's his), and I get it only as long as I have a perfect record. Help me, please.

Buzzy

Dear Buzzy:

Tell that shy octopus that 40 eyes are of no value unless the driver's two hands and two feet are free to act in a split second. Give her these alternatives: Either she stays over on her side of the seat or you'll both have to travel by bus or be pedestrians.

Of all regularly published columns, advice columns have the largest number of regular readers. Why? Some say it's like peeking through a window. As we read the problem, we feel as if we're intruding on someone else's life, and that gives us satisfaction. Others say that by recognizing our own problems in other people's situations, we are helped by both the question and the answer.

People certainly have a variety of reasons for writing for advice to a person they don't know. And we have a variety of reasons for reading the advice given. If you like to read advice columns, you might be especially interested in this project.

Read and save the columns for a few months. Keep track of the subject matter of each letter. For example, you will probably find that many letters have to do with getting along with people, so perhaps "people" could be one major heading. But what people? Relatives, boyfriends, girl friends, employers, fellow workers, family members?

Why did the person write? What was the problem? Did it involve money matters, sex, etiquette, hurt feelings? Does the person writing seem to be liberal or conservative? Old or young? Male or female? Are there any categories of people who seem more prone to write for advice than others?

Analyzing the problems and the people involved can be very interesting. Do you think the people who write for advice represent average Americans? Or do you think they are all nuts? Do you think the problems are very common and human? Or do you think they are peculiar and unusual?

Another approach is to question several people you know on a certain problem you find in an advice column. For example:

"Dear _____:
"There are a number of small children who live next door to us. We like to be friendly with our neighbors, but these children continually ring our doorbell and ask to come in. If we don't answer the door, they peek in the windows and follow us around the house by looking through the windows.

*"I've told their mother about this but she just
says, 'Send the children home.' What should we
do now?"*

Whatever kind of problem you select, be sure to ask a variety of people for their reactions. Record the age, sex, family
status (parent, child, etc.), occupation and political leanings of
your respondents. Then compare their answers with the columnist's advice. Can you draw any conclusions about the problem? Is it universal? Does it elicit sympathy? Scorn? Confusion?
Interest? And what about the columnist? Does the advice seem
to be in line with how most people feel? Or does it seem to
reflect the values of only a certain kind of person?

For display and analysis, you might consider laying out your
research in the following way:

Question—

Columnist's answer—

My answer—

Respondents

Name, age, political leanings	Family status	Occupation	Excerpts from answer
Mr. X, 53 years old, liberal Republican	Father of 4, Grandfather of 6	Self-employed carpenter	(1) How old are the kids? (2) If they're under three, take them by the hand and bring them home. (3) If they're older, give them a swat and send them home.

19

2

AND NOW A WORD FROM OUR SPONSOR

To which companies do the following advertising slogans belong?

It's the real thing.
Let your fingers do the walking.
Get your hands on a . . ., you'll never let go.
Coming through.
Building a better way to see the U.S.A.

If your answer is the Coca-Cola Company, the Yellow Pages, Toyota, Chrysler and Chevrolet, you are a good listener and have demonstrated what advertisers want most: to get people to remember the names of their products.

But many people can't remember product names, even though they can whistle the tune that goes with the product's slogan. This gives advertisers fits, and millions of dollars are spent trying to figure out how to plant the product so firmly in the buyer's mind that he'll buy it when he goes to the store.

You might spend some time evaluating the effectiveness of advertising campaigns. Make a slogan questionnaire and ask people to identify the product that goes with the slogan. If the slogans are part of a musical jingle, you might play a tape recording of both the music and the slogan with the product's name "bleeped out." Or you might try one approach with one group of people and the other approach with a different group and so be able to judge which part of a commercial makes the greatest impression, the words or the music.

Another interesting possibility is to estimate the effectiveness of advertising directed at children. Get up early some Saturday morning and listen to the toy and cereal commercials on TV. Then test your brothers and sisters and some of the younger children in your neighborhood. Do they remember the product that goes with the slogan? Do they pester parents to buy what they see on TV? You might make an expedition to your local supermarket and see the effect that children's demands have on their mothers' purchasing habits. Are advertisers hitting the mark when they beam their messages directly at children?

When doing this project, keep a record of the age and occupation of your respondents. A man working for an automobile company probably will recognize car commercials, because he has an interest in them. A housewife probably will be able to identify detergent commercials, etc.

Does the effectiveness of an advertiser's campaign have a direct relationship to sales? Figures are available to help you determine this. Ask your local librarians how to go about getting them.

3

INFORMATION
RETRIEVAL

One of the fascinating things about modern life is the speed with which information can be obtained. Tape recordings, video tape and teletype make it possible to store information until it's needed by television and radio stations and newspapers. Computers play a major role in this process, and the system which produces information on demand is usually called information retrieval.

The retrieval system described here is the same as one type of computer operation. But instead of an expensive card-sorting machine, you can use an ice pick.

Any retrieval system is only as good as the information stored in it. Let's say there's been a water-main break at the intersection of Martin and Rowan streets. Both these streets are dead ends. The school bus can't get the children home at the usual time. The school principal wants his secretary to call and warn all the parents on Martin and Rowan streets. How can the secretary get the necessary information as quickly as possible?

With information stored on cards such as the one in the illustration, the secretary will have an easy time of it. Each card stands for a student. Each possible description has a hole next to it. But only details that apply to John Q. Jones have wedges cut into the holes. Looking at the wedges, you can see that John Q. Jones is in kindergarten, lives on Martin Street, has

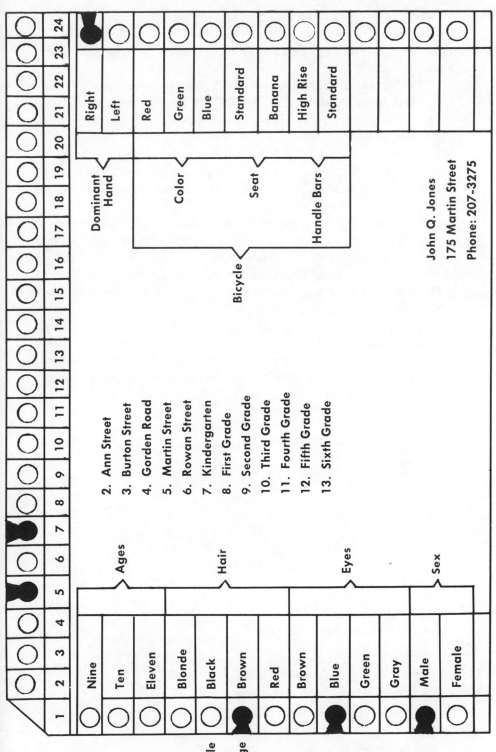

brown hair, blue eyes and is male. He is right-handed and does not own a bicycle.

The secretary then has to push the ice pick into the hole marked Martin Street, and shake. All the Martin Street cards will drop out. Since kindergarten children go home early, their parents should be called first. She can push the pick into the kindergarten slot of the Martin Street cards, and shake. John Q. Jones's card will drop out, along with all the other kindergarteners on Martin Street. Now she has the names, addresses and phone numbers she needs.

To make your own information retrieval cards, put down as many characteristics as you want. Punch holes for every number that identifies a characteristic. Cut wedges in the holes that apply to the particular person the card describes. Now you can insert an ice pick to find out the groups of people who have one characteristic in common.

Can you think of ways this kind of information retrieval system can be used by businesses such as insurance companies? Can you think of information a storekeeper, doctor, service-station operator, florist or farmer might want to store? Would an information retrieval system be of use to your family in any way?

4

DISCRIMINATION AS PREJUDICE

Since the early 1960's Americans have become increasingly aware of discrimination and its effects on people involved. Although the word has several meanings, this project uses the word discrimination to mean "different treatment" because of race, religion, national origin, sex or age. Not all discrimination is bad—children under the age of sixteen are not allowed to drive for reasons of strength, size and maturity. But when there is no reason for discrimination except the race, religion, national origin, age or sex of the person, we say that the "different treatment" is motivated by prejudice.

You can study discrimination in a number of ways.

One way is by time comparison. Compare advertisements in a magazine of the early 1960's with one today. How many black people are in the ads?

You can make a careful study of a presentation on TV. Does the program or the advertisement make one race or sex or age group seem superior or inferior to others?

Another way to examine discrimination and its impact is to study the effect of discrimination on you because of your age. List all of the things you can't do because of your age. List all of the phrases that remind you of your difference: "When you get older," "It won't be long now," "My, how you've grown!" Write down how you feel about being treated as a kid. Just to be fair, ask your mom and dad to do the same thing from their point of view. How does it feel *not* to be a kid anymore —they have to pay the full price for movies, they have to work, etc.

After you've made these several studies, you might want to consider the following questions:

(1) What examples of discrimination have you identified?
(2) To what extent does this discrimination seem motivated by prejudice?
(3) To what extent does discrimination on the basis of prejudice seem to be disappearing?
(4) In the case where the discrimination and/or prejudice is practiced against you, how do you feel about it?

Finally, of all the types of discrimination mentioned, consider that your age will change—you will grow up. Discrimination on the basis of your age will then stop. But no other characteristic against which there is discrimination can change. How do you think the people affected feel about that?

5

FIND A REPLACEMENT
—PART I

Man always seems to want to improve what he has—to replace a good product with a more-bounce-to-the-ounce, better-quality-for-less-money item. How does this tendency affect you and your family?

Choose something from a wide variety of products—a washing machine, silverware, a cleaning product, a vacuum cleaner, a piece of furniture, a bicycle. Write down the size, weight, serial number (if any), the manufacturer and an exact description of the product.

Armed with this information, visit stores that sell this product. Better yet, visit the store that sold your family the original item. Ask the store owner, manager or the department manager if the item is available. Be sure to tell him that you are not a potential customer but rather, a student of "product turnover."

Look at the product he's selling and check it against your specifications. Ask him if the materials used in his product are the same as materials in yours or if the product is a "new, improved" version.

You can follow up your findings by writing to manufacturers. For a product that is no longer available, find out how long it lasted, when production was stopped and why. For a product that has changed, ask how long the "new, improved" version

27

has been on the market and if there are any plans for further changes. You might also ask the manufacturer whether he is replacing products more rapidly than he did ten years ago. What is the "production lifetime" of a refrigerator, a pickup truck, a radio, a sewing machine, a power tool? Your findings should provide interesting information on the way our economy works.

6

FIND A REPLACEMENT —PART II

How often does your mother use her vacuum cleaner? When was the last time she bought a new one? When was the last time your family bought a new refrigerator? A new pair of shoes? Does your father buy a new car every year? A new wallet? A new electric razor?

Thinking about these questions might give you some idea about *why* manufacturers change and/or improve their products. Choose a wide variety of items in your home—toys, washing machine, can opener, cooking utensils, radios, lawn mowers, etc. Ask the following questions:

(1) How old is the product?
(2) Who uses it?
(3) How often is it used?
(4) Was the product bought to replace an older model?

Now for some other ideas: Are the older products used more frequently than the newer products? Has the use changed as the product has gotten older? How many products, such as toys, aren't used at all? Are the newer products significantly different from older products of the same type? If the product is a replacement, what did it replace? Is the replacement a "new, improved" model or just more recently manufactured than the older model?

Note when each product was purchased and calculated its average "lifetime." How long does a radio or a TV or a tea kettle last in your house? How do your findings compare with what you learned about "production lifetime" in Find A Replacement—Part I?

Can you make any generalizations about why and when your family buys a replacement? Do your family's buying habits give you any clues about why manufacturers change or improve their products?

7

FIND A REPLACEMENT –PART III

One of the major influences on our country's economy is the automobile industry. If a large number of new cars is sold each year, large amounts of rubber, metal, plastic and glass will be needed to manufacture them. Large numbers of people will be employed. These people will spend the money they make on other goods and services, and an observer might say that the economy looks pretty healthy.

Out of these facts come certain charges, some of which are true, some half true and some false. One is that American-made cars are not built to last. Another is that American car makers change body styles frequently to encourage the public to buy the latest model.

You can conduct studies to test these beliefs, at least in your own town. First, test for durability. A good approach here might be to spend several hours at a busy gas station. Get the owner's permission to stay there and record the *make* and *year* of each car that stops. If you really know your automobiles, you can gather the same information by standing on a busy street corner. But good luck at guessing the year of a Volkswagen!

After you get a good sampling (we suggest a minimum of 200 cars), figure out which manufacturer seems to have the largest number of old cars still on the road.

SOCIAL SCIENCE PROJECTS YOU CAN DO

The next step is to study how much car styles have changed over the years. Local car dealers might be able to supply pictures of models they have sold for, say, the last ten or fifteen years. Which manufacturers seem to change styles the most? Which the least? Ask the dealers if these style changes affect sales. Did they affect sales more in the past than they do now? Also (in line with your durability test above), ask the dealer how much it costs a year to service various model cars.

Now compare cars by price. The most inexpensive American cars are priced to compete with foreign imports such as Toyotas, Volkswagens and Fiats. Compare the American and foreign cars for style changes, durability and resale value. *Consumer Reports* magazine will help you compare the mechanical features. Make the same comparisons for medium- and high-priced cars. What do you think? Do American models stand up to the competition?

8

TIME

Most people are conscious of time. On a superhighway, they will speed up to pass the car in front of them, and then immediately slow down to turn off at their exit. How much time did they save by passing that car? Three seconds, ten seconds? And how many times do people go through a traffic light just as it's turning red? How much time did they really save by cutting it close? Twenty seconds?

The purpose of this project is to investigate whether or not we're all a little time-crazy. Begin by examining all the ways time is impressed upon you, starting with things like, "Hurry up, Joan! Put down that social science projects book or you'll be late for school." Write down everything anyone says to you about time. Include sounds, too, like the noon whistle or school bell. Compare a school day to a nonschool day.

Next, think over your reactions to time. Are you an impatient person? If so, you're probably concerned with time. Do you get upset if other people are late? Are *you* always on time? Compare your attitudes with others.

Consider making a time-interest survey of certain groups of people. Start with your classroom. How many students check their watches or the clock during a specific period? How often does the teacher check his watch or clock? If you live near a subway or a train or a bus line, go to the station and observe the people. How many check watches, look at clocks or ask the time while they are waiting? Do you think knowing the time will get them to their destination any faster? Make the same survey at a busy intersection, a supermarket, a bowling alley. Does a specific activity seem to affect a person's interest in time? Listen to several radio stations. How often does each announcer tell the time?

34

After making this study, you might compare the results with your findings from such projects as Rhythms, Pressure or "On Hold" in Modern Life. Does our concern for time have something to do with the patterns in our lives?

9

FAMILY MOBILITY

Mobility is a major feature of American life, both past and present. Our earliest settlers pulled up stakes in Europe to come here. Since the early 1600's, more and more people immigrated to America while more and more Americans pushed west toward the Pacific Ocean. Usually these moves were motivated by hopes for religious freedom, freedom from persecution, a better life, wealth, social or individual status.

What moves has your family made and why? You can trace this in several ways. Begin with your mother and father. Where did they grow up? Where did they live before you were born? Where have you lived?

Now you can work back to your grandparents and great-grandparents. Use a map and a chart to keep track of where everyone moved. Did your grandparents move more frequently than your parents? Are there any geographic patterns to the moves? For instance, was your family part of the great westward migration? Were any of the moves related to major events in American history such as the Depression? World War II? Does your family mobility tend to be spread over wide areas or to be concentrated in only a few? Can you find out why your family moved as it did? Can you notice any interesting trends such as one generation moving from the city to a farm, a later generation moving from the farm back to a city, and still a later generation going from the city to the suburbs or rural areas? How would you explain this kind of sequence? Compare the information you gather about your family with the information available from the U.S. Census Bureau. Are your family patterns similar to national patterns?

An alternative to working back through generations is to examine just one generation such as your parents and all their brothers and sisters. At one point these brothers and sisters lived together. Where do they live now? Why has Uncle Edgar moved all over the country while Uncle George lives down the block from where he was born?

Once you have acquired this information, you might want to display it on a map or chart. Different color inks can represent different generations, different branches of your family and the national patterns. And on some holiday like Christmas or Thanksgiving or a family anniversary when you all get together, you'll have an interested audience to whom you can present your research.

10

SWEARING INDEX

A recent study at a major university indicated that one word out of seven spoken by construction workers was a profane or swear word. The same study reported that college students sprinkled their speech with one swear word for every fourteen words spoken.

How about starting a swearing index to rate your friends and acquaintances? First, you'll have to decide what you're indexing. What is profanity? What is swearing?

The dictionary offers some general guidelines but is not particularly helpful with specifics. Swearing is defined as using profane, blasphemous or obscene language. Profane is characterized as defiling something holy. Blasphemous means impiously irreverent. Obscene refers to inciting lust, depravity or indecency.

Ask a sampling of people what they think swearing is. You'll probably come up with a variety of answers. As an example, at one time "damn" and "hell" were not used on television. Now they are. Other four-letter words are regularly used in movies and on stage, but not on TV. Do you think this is an indication that ideas about "bad" language are changing? Are they changing in your town?

Your mission, then, should you choose to accept it, is to define swearing and set about finding out how much people swear.

SOCIAL SCIENCE PROJECTS YOU CAN DO

The best way to get information is to record conversations on tape. Afterwards, count the total number of words spoken by a person and figure the swear words as a percent of that total.

If you don't have access to a tape recorder, scribble down what you hear as best you can. Try to get in on the conversations of various groups. For instance, compare the amount of swearing in the boys' locker room, a bowling alley, the school cafeteria, a supermarket. Do boys swear more than girls? Do high school girls swear more than junior high girls? Children more than parents? Who swears more at each other: girls against boys, adults against children, fathers against mothers? How much did your personal swearing index jump while you were trying to complete this project?

11

NATURE AND SOCIETY—PART I

"This is one of the worst winters we've ever had!" How many times have you heard that statement without really exploring its meaning? Does the speaker mean there was too little snow or too much? Does the speaker own a ski resort or is he a government official? In one case, snow is money in the bank. In the other, it's a headache and overtime pay for the workers who clear snow-clogged streets.

The purpose of this project is to research and evaluate the impact of nature on people who live in an industrialized economy. With a heavy snowfall, for instance, try to trace all its good and bad consequences. Apart from skiing and snow removal, what are some others?

(1) Call the hospital or a local doctor and ask if heavy snow contributes to an increase in heart attacks as people try to shovel out. Are there more deaths because of delays in getting medical attention?

(2) Call the local water authority and ask what impact a heavy snow has on the community's water supply. When the ground is frozen, is snow better for the water supply than rain?

(3) Call or write to a city agency along any local river and ask if they have to prepare for possible flooding when the snow melts.

(4) Call or write to insurance agents and ask how snow affects accident rates and insurance claims.

(5) Ask a psychiatrist if heavy snow seems to influence the mood of his patients.

(6) Call or write to a farmer to get his reactions.

(7) Find out how snow affects your grandparents. Is there any difference between your father's reaction to snow and your little sister's?

You can think of many other people to interview, and when you're satisfied that you have enough information, arrange it in a social cost/social gain chart. List the good and the bad results of a heavy snow. Use statistics to support your findings. For instance, how many heart attacks? How much water in the reservoir?

Now what do you think? Is snow "good" or "bad"?

12

NATURE AND SOCIETY—PART II

Today people are becoming more aware of the relationship between man and nature. You might want to explore this development further by analyzing the impact of a natural act on man or the impact of a man-made act on both nature and man. Take, for example, a new road. By interviewing and writing to a variety of people you can begin to see how many people and places this single event affects. Consider the following:

(1) Will more cars be going into a city or resort area because of a new or better road?

(2) What will be the impact on that city or resort?

(3) What will happen to the land around the new road? Will the road building and the increased auto traffic affect plant and animal life? Your local Audubon Society or conservation commission might provide some useful information on this question.

(4) If the road goes through a town or city, how many houses or buildings had to be torn down to make room for it? What happened to the people who were displaced?

(5) How will the road affect the people who live near it? You might want to measure noise and air pollution levels on the road. You might also want to talk to a real-estate agent about land values.

41

(6) Does the new road bypass a town? If so, what are the effects on that town's industry and commerce?

(7) Very often when large areas of land are paved over, water runoff from rain and snow poses a problem. There are fewer trees and less soil to soak up the water. You might want to investigate what steps the road builder took to solve this problem. If there is flooding, how does it affect the surrounding area?

You can think of many other possible questions. After you are satisfied with your findings, consider making a large diagram to explain your research. You might draw a road. Then, using arrows, point to the areas this road will affect. Then, using another kind of line, show how the people in the affected areas have reacted to (or are likely to react to) the road.

For instance, if you have reason to believe that people will move away from the road, draw an arrow from the road to the affected residential area. Draw broken lines to the areas where the people are likely to move. How do you think these new areas would be affected by an influx of people?

By the time you're finishing diagraming the results of your findings, your picture will probably look like a web. It might be very worthwhile to show this picture to several different kinds of people and institutions: the mayor, a local conservation group, businessmen, home owners, the board of education. What are their reactions to your findings? How alert are they to nature-society relationships?

13

NATURE AND SOCIETY—PART III

Another way of looking at the relationship between man and nature is to consider some of the activities of man that require cooperation from nature for their success. We've already explored the impact of snow on the owner of a ski area.

You might explore the impact of natural events on the following businesses and areas:

(1) Does rainy weather in Europe hurt the airline industry in the summer?

(2) Does a lack of snow in the Northeast help the airlines in flying people to Europe and to the Rockies?

(3) Call or write a motel owner in New England, Pennsylvania or Colorado and ask about the economics of the fall-foliage season. Is a fall weekend any different from a winter ski weekend?

(4) Call or write resort owners and ask about their problems with nature in the summer. Can too much sunny weather be as bad for business as too much rain?

(5) What effect does a rainy summer have on the home-construction industry?

(6) Can weather influence tourist trade in a city? Write

a New York restaurant owner and ask about the impact on his business of a rainy Thanksgiving weekend.

(7) In your own school, study attendance figures and see if the weather influences attendance. Compare grade school with junior high and high school. Consider the effect of a severe cold spell; a heavy rainstorm; a snowstorm, assuming school is open; the first real spring day.

You might also compare student attitudes toward the weather and its influences. After each of the events mentioned in item #7, ask students if they are happy and then ask their reaction to the weather. Then ask, if they could, would they travel somewhere else—a ski resort, a beach, the city, etc. Some of their attitudes probably will reflect the views that influence the income of owners of restaurants and resorts.

14

TAXING QUESTION

The Internal Revenue Service designs the federal income tax forms. It also issues a booklet that explains how to fill out these forms.

The instructions on the latest forms and in the latest booklet are supposed to be so clear and simple that most taxpayers should not need an expert to fill them out. We've also heard that if a taxpayer takes a "standard deduction," even a fifth grader could fill out the forms properly.

Although you might not be in the fifth grade, you might try to fill out a form. To make this a real test, get two or three of your friends to fill out forms (using the same financial information) and then compare the results. Be sure to get a copy of the illustrated tax booklet so that you'll have all the help you'll need. Now try something like this:

John Citizen and his wife, Jane, are both 39 years old. They have two children, Michael (age 17) and Michele (age 14). John is an income-tax consultant. He lives with his family in an eight-room house. He uses one of the rooms as his business office.

Last year John earned $18,000 from his consulting business. He had $1,200 additional income from renting his small lakefront cottage, valued at $15,000. He had no other income and spent no money for the maintenance of his homes.

John bought a car for his wife last year, on which he makes monthly payments of $97, of which $20 per month is interest. The mortgage payments on his home come to $175 a month, of which $140 is interest. The cottage is all paid up.

John traveled 22,000 miles in his business last year and another 12,000 miles for pleasure. He doesn't smoke or drink and the entire family had no medical expenses last year.

John lives in a small town in New Jersey. He did not have to pay state income tax but his state property taxes totaled $1,650.

Based on the information given, see what you and your friends think John and Jane Citizen owe the Internal Revenue Service. While using the tax form and tax guide, keep track of the directions that seem difficult to interpret and the words you have to look up. How many times did you and your friends have to ask for help? Did the people you asked have any trouble figuring out the answer? Do you think there's any future in becoming a tax consultant?

15

RECALL

In December, 1971, General Motors announced that it was recalling more than six million Chevrolets and light trucks manufactured between 1965 and 1969. The recall involved a motor mount that might break when the car accelerated, causing the engine to tip backward and the car to speed up. At the same time, the brake lines would be damaged so that the driver could not stop the car except by turning off the ignition.

This project involves finding out all you can about recalls. Begin by going through old newspapers. (Your local librarian can tell you the most efficient and effective way to conduct this research.) Look for information about who initiated the recall —the manufacturer, a watchdog agency such as the National Safety Council or a private individual or group. How was the problem first discovered? What did the manufacturer have to

say about the problem? What steps were taken to remedy the situation?

Then select the recall campaigns that interest you most and dig in. In the case of a car recall, read and write to several motor magazines and find out what they know about the situation. Then you could go to the local dealer and ask questions such as:

(1) Who initiated the recall?

(2) How many cars in this area were involved?

(3) How was the defect uncovered? Did you have complaints prior to the recall? How many?

(4) What did you have to do to correct the problem?

(5) How much did it cost to fix each car?

(6) Did the manufacturer replace the defective part? Or did it install a compensating device?

(7) In your judgment, were the repaired cars as safe as a car that never had this probelm?

(8) Who paid for the repairs, both labor and parts?

(9) How long did it take to repair each car?

(10) Can you give me the names of some customers who were affected? (If the car dealer won't give you any names, ask around. Maybe your parents or teachers know someone who was involved in the recall.)

Questions for the car owner:

(1) Did you know about the defective part before the recall was announced to the public?

(2) How were you notified?

(3) How long did it take to repair your car?

(4) What means of transportation did you use while your car was being repaired?

(5) How do you feel about having your car recalled?

(6) Are you satisfied with the repair work? Do you think your car is safe? Do you still own the car?

(7) Did the repair work cost you anything?

(8) Would you buy another car from this manufacturer?

48

16

GUN CONTROL

It has been estimated that a new handgun is sold in the United States every thirteen seconds. Used guns are said to be traded at a rate of one every two minutes. A Remington deer rifle, the type used to kill Martin Luther King, costs approximately $265. An Ivers Johnson pistol like the one that killed Robert F. Kennedy costs $6.00.

If you are interested in guns, you might consider the issue of gun control as a potential project. The Federal Gun Control law of 1968, among other provisions, bans mail-order purchase of rifles, shotguns, handguns and ammunition and curbs out-of-state buying of such items.

But in spite of the law, the number of guns available to private citizens has increased. Your project might be to research (1) the availability of guns in your area, (2) how many private citizens in your neighborhood own guns and for what reason, and (3) how the man on the street feels about gun-control legislation. Do older people tend to favor gun controls? What about college students? Is there a difference in opinion between men and women? What about people of different income levels?

To begin, study a copy of the Gun Control law. (Write to your senators or congressman for a copy.) Does it seem strong enough? Too strong? Do you think it is easy to enforce? What seem to be its most important features?

49

Next, you can go to a store that sells guns and ask the owner or manager a series of questions such as:

(1) How old must a person be to purchase a gun?
(2) Is any identification necessary?
(3) Which is easier to buy—a rifle or a handgun?
(4) Who buys your guns?
(5) Do you sell more guns at certain times of the year?
(6) Can a gun be purchased through the mail?
(7) What kinds of guns are most popular in this community?

Then you can head for the local police station and find out how the police feel about guns. Are guns a problem in the community? Are the police active in enforcing the gun control law? Do they keep track of who owns guns in your town? How do they feel about the federal law? How many crimes or accidents involving guns were there last year?

Here are some questions you might ask your neighbors:

(1) Do you own any guns? How many?
(2) What kinds of guns are they?
(3) Who uses the guns?
(4) What are they used for?
(5) When was the last time a gun was fired?
(6) Do you have any trouble buying ammunition?
(7) Do you feel there should be laws controlling the sale of guns and ammunition? Why? Why not?
(8) Should a private citizen be required to have a license for the guns he owns or plans to purchase? Why? Why not?
(9) If law-enforcement agencies did their work better, do you feel that gun-control laws would be necessary? Why? Why not?

You might also seek out local or regional groups for their opinions of guns. The Chamber of Commerce, the American Legion, the Audubon Society and various conservation and wild-life societies are good possibilities.

With all this information in hand, you should be able to make some reasonably solid generalizations about the need for gun-control in your town, the pros and cons of gun control and the effectiveness of existing legislation. Your school will probably be interested in the results of your findings.

17

LANGUAGE AND SOCIETY

Many of the words and phrases we use everyday are clichés or colloquialisms. "He's feeling his oats," and "He's in orbit" essentially mean the same thing. The difference is that one phrase comes from our agricultural past and the other is a product of our space age.

The purpose of this project is to analyze common phrases—their meanings, their use and their origin. What clichés do you and your friends use? From where did these phrases originate? Space? Agriculture? Drugs? Music? Comic strips? Ethnic groups? Government agencies? Comedians? Orators? Authors?

You might also compare your clichés with those used by adults. Is there a generation gap in language? Does your dad "mow the back forty" more than he does his "own thing"? Does your teacher tell you "never look a gift horse in the mouth" more than she says "get yourself together"?

You could also take one word like "bomb" and examine its different meanings. You throw "bombs" on the football field. You "bomb" a test (which at times has meant both doing well and doing badly). The movie was a "bomb." The actress who starred in it was a "bombshell."

How long does a phrase stay in fashion? Is it dead for you by the time your mother starts using it? Are newspapers and magazines "up" on the latest words? What about television?

Try getting together a list of phrases that you think are particularly expressive or popular and see how many people actually use them and how often. Can you think of reasons why a particular person uses particular clichés?

18

SIGNS OF THE TIMES

In 1965, Congress enacted the federal Highway Beautification Act. Under its terms, approximately 600,000 road signs (mostly along interstate highways) were declared illegal.

However, to certain citizen groups enforcement of this law has been painfully slow; armed with chain saws, they began cutting down the illegal signs at the rate of six a day. Notes left by the chain-saw "phantoms" indicated that they were tired of waiting for the government to rid the landscape of the unwanted and illegal signs.

In the meantime, representatives of the Department of Transportation indicated that the government did not intend to destroy the billboard industry, but rather to remove all billboards from residential, rural, recreational and commercial centers on interstate and federally-funded highways.

What does all of this mean? Is the Highway Beautification Act really being enforced? Are signs being taken down in your area? If removal seems to be going slowly, can you think of any reasons why? (In Maine, it is estimated that removing one sign will cost at least $10,000.) What is the procedure for sign removal?

To find out all you can about the Highway Beautification Act, write to the Secretary of Transportation, U.S. Department of Transportation, Washington, D.C. 20590. He may be able to send you a copy of the bill and give you some information about sign removal in your area. Your senators and congressman are also possible sources of information.

To find out some of the problems of sign owners, jot down the name of the company that owns signs which seem to be illegal according to the terms of the law. (You can usually find the owner's name at the bottom of the sign's frame.) Then telephone or write to the owner.

With a particular sign in mind, ask a series of questions such as:

(1) Is this sign in violation of the Highway Beautification Act of 1965?
(2) Have any public officials or private citizens contacted you about removing the sign?
(3) Are your signs insured against vandalism?
(4) What plans do you have for removing illegal signs?
(5) How has the Beautification Act affected business?

In surveying your area, it might also be interesting to note whether local and national politicians are using illegal billboards in their campaigns. Are these politicians aware of the Beautification Act?

19

MODERN-DAY
RIP VAN WINKLE

Soldier Shoichi Yokoi came home from World War II on February 5, 1972. Rather than surrender to his American enemy, he had hid out in the Guam jungles for the last twenty-eight years. He survived on breadfruit, coconuts, snails, rats' livers, shrimps and frogs. He made his clothes from tree bark and kept track of the time by marking a tree trunk every full moon.

After having made 336 marks on the tree, Yokoi, now fifty-six years old, got his first look at his homeland since the war. What did he see? Newspaper accounts of Yokoi's "surrender" indicate that he cried when he saw Mount Fuji and that thousands of people gave him a hero's welcome as he stepped off the plane. But now that Yokoi is home, what practical problems do you think he faces? How much have things changed?

This project suggests that you put yourself in Yokoi's place. Imagine that you have been in solitary confinement for the last twenty-eight years and have just returned home to your family and friends.

Is your town much different than it was twenty-eight years ago? Has modern earth-moving equipment remade the landscape? Are the rivers and lakes in the same place they always were? (One town in northwestern Connecticut completely disappeared in the last twenty-eight years. The area is now a reservoir.)

What about the school you went to twenty-eight years ago? Is it still there? Is the church still there? The corner store? Does your family have many more appliances now? If you wore the same clothes today that you used to wear twenty-eight years ago, would people think you looked like a freak?

Also think about the changes you'd face in your personal life. Would you be able to live with your family? How about your friends? How would they react to you? What would you do for a living?

To carry out this project, you'll have to consult with people who lived in your town while you were away. What changes have they noticed? Back issues of the local newspaper will give you some information about your Rip van Winkle period.

Now imagine that you fell asleep (while reading this book) and will wake up in 1990. What changes would you anticipate? Visit your town or city hall and ask your local planners if any plans have been made for the future. What population growth do they anticipate? Where do they expect new houses, businesses and civic installations to be built? Will the school system be set up the same way it is now? Will the transportation system be the same? Do you think you'd like to live in your town in the year 1990?

20

WHAT'S IN A NAME?

Along with fingerprints and personality, your name makes you unique. It helps to make you an individual in the eyes of society. Few of you are likely to change your name. Once you become an adult you could, if you wish, have your name officially changed. When a girl marries she can add her husband's name to her own. But with these exceptions, most names last a lifetime. Since you have to live with it, why not find out something about your "label"?

One project might be to find out the meaning of your name. First names often go back to ancient times and many have Hebrew origins with biblical meanings. (One of the authors of this book has a first name that means world ruler.) Did your parents know what your name meant when they gave it to you?

Last names, also known as surnames or family names, are more recent in origin. Most evolved in the Middle Ages and referred to the family's occupation or other circumstances. Cooper, for instance, probably comes from the German word, Küfer, which means barrelmaker. Check the national origin of your name and try to find out its original spelling. Many people, when they came to this country, gave their names an English spelling to make it easier to pronounce.

Another project might be to investigate whether or not your first and middle names have been handed down from previous generations. Are you named after a relative? A friend of the family? A month of the year? A national hero? What are some of the name patterns and practices in your family? You might want to compare your family's history of names with some of your friends'. Be alert to possible differences in the way various ethnic groups use names. If there are foreign students in your school, interview them about names in their countries. If you were introduced to Chiang Kai-shek, would you call him Mr. Kai-shek? Mr. Chiang?

21

HAPPINESS IS...

What is happiness? Probably everyone you know has a different definition. But are there some ideas of happiness that most of us have in common?

This project asks you to pinpoint concepts of happiness that Americans seem to share. One indicator is TV commercials.

Every advertiser wants to sell his product. He may have only thirty or sixty seconds to get his message across, and in that time he wants us to feel good about his product. So he's likely to try to associate it with something he thinks will make us happy. For instance, a commercial for dandruff shampoo might go something like this:

> Scene 1. Girl sitting at dressing table combing her hair. Mother standing nearby.
> Girl: Oh Mother! What am I going to do? Bob will never ask me to marry him if he sees this terrible dandruff!
> Mother: Darling, you should try Dappy Doink Dandruff Shampoo. Wash your hair three times a week with Dappy Doink Dandruff Shampoo and your dandruff problems will disappear.

Scene II. Girl in wedding dress standing outside church, surrounded by people throwing rice. Mother kissing her on the cheek.
Girl: My wedding day—thanks to Dappy Doink Dandruff Shampoo!

Consider this possible commercial: A handsome young man with a cigar clamped between his teeth. He rides. He lassos mustangs. He smokes. He jokes. There's a hint of serious determination about him. Everyone loves him. He's a man. And if he's *your* idea of a man, you will probably have good feelings about this kind of commercial.

Study TV commercials to discover what values sponsors think will make us happy. Is the sponsor promoting comfort, leisure, success, thrift, adventure, social acceptability, cleanliness, sexiness, femininity, masculinity, youth? Once you've identified the values and the products, you are ready to begin gathering data for your study.

Interview a variety of people to find out whether a goal such as masculinity or femininity is really important to them. Then try to determine what your subjects mean by masculinity and femininity. Find out if the people you interview feel that drinking beer, or smoking cigars or driving a big car is an indication of masculinity. Is taking a bubble bath or wearing the latest type of clothes an indication of femininity? Do the answers you receive seem to be related to the age, sex, occupation or income of the respondents?

61

Another approach to this project is to find out if a person uses a certain product and why.

Example:

Q: Do you drink _____ cola?
A: Yes.
Q: Why?
A: Because I like it.
Q: Do you like the way it tastes?
Q: Have you compared _____ cola with other colas?
Q: Can you remember the TV commercial that promotes _____ cola?
Q: Are there any particular times when you enjoy drinking _____ cola?
Q: What's your impression of the company that makes _____ cola?

If the person you're interviewing gives answers that relate to the advertiser's message, then that message has gotten through. The advertiser has successfully associated his product with something that gives this person pleasure.

After working on this project for a while, you might select the products that appeal to you on the basis of advertisements. Why do you like these products? Are they really better than competitors' products?

22

COMPARING THE NEWS REPORTS

At one point in our history, we learned the news from only two sources: newspapers and word of mouth. And in many cases the person telling the news had read it in a newspaper. So, in effect, the newspaper was our only form of mass communication, of sending information quickly to large numbers of people.

In this century, three other forms of mass communication were introduced: the weekly news magazine, which reports the news and comments on it; radio, a new form of word of mouth; and television. Now you can use all four sources of information to learn what's happening in the world. The purpose of this project is to compare the media and determine for yourself which serves you best.

This comparison can be made in several ways. TV news programs last about a half hour, although in some areas there is a half hour of local news followed by a half hour of national and international news. You'll probably want to watch the full program. Then spend an hour listening to the radio news. Read a newspaper for an hour; devote another hour to a news magazine. You may want to spread out your research over a few days. Then consider the following: Which medium did you enjoy the most? From which do you think you learned the most?

You might also want to compare the reporting of a single story. Select an event on which all four media report. Compare the coverage for completeness—information included and time given to the topic (for newspapers and magazines, time spent reading the story). You can do the same thing with TV news specials and with feature stories in news magazines.

Once you have your comparisons, ask yourself some questions. Is one medium enough to keep a person informed on current events? How are the medias different? How are they the same? Can you rely on two, for instance, and forget about the other two? See what your parents and teachers think about your conclusions.

23

CONTAINER SURVEY

Today people are more and more concerned about environmental problems. We worry about air pollution from factory smokestacks, incinerators and automobiles; water pollution from factory and human waste and just plain litter. This project suggests that you investigate the litter situation in your town, starting with bottles and cans.

Walk around your neighborhood looking for discarded bottles and cans. Using a street map, record where you found the objects and how many there were. Mark the spot on the map, but you'll need a sheet of paper to record the amount. Your record system might read: Corner Martin and Smith streets, 5D (on the map)—5 bottles, 16 cans. Hopefully you won't find much litter at all. But if there seems to be a concentration in several places, try to find out why.

Observe several of these high-density areas for a few weeks. Is the trash dumped at night? Find out by checking the area in the late afternoon and then again early in the morning. Is there a soft-drink machine nearby? Are there enough litter baskets in the area?

65

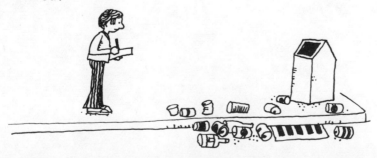

Once you have gathered information, you could contact your local newspaper. A reporter might be interested in using your information as the basis of a story about keeping your town clean. You should also find out if your town has an ordinance against littering. Should one be proposed? (See Government in Action, Part II.) Is anyone clearing away the rubbish in the high-density areas? (See Government in Action, Part I.)

You might also find out if bottle companies pay for the return of empties. Does a local civic group or Boy Scout troop have a recycling project? Can they be encouraged to start one? Try to think of additional ways in which littering could be stopped. Your study, if done carefully and accurately, could be very important.

24

ON THE MOVE—
PART I

Historically Americans have always been on the move. The nineteenth century saw Americans traveling across the Appalachian Mountains all the way to the Pacific Ocean. In 1900, many people believed that once the West was densely populated, Americans might stop moving. Here's a project to check the validity of that belief.

First, ask your parents for a picture of your kindergarten or first-grade class. If you didn't live in your present town when you were in the first grade, ask a friend for his class picture. Now make a record of how many people have left and how many have joined your class since the first grade. If possible, find out the year each person came or went. In this way you can figure out the average number of people moving in and out of your town every year, or the rate of mobility of your town.

Consider making a comparison with other periods. For example, for the year 1915, find out who the first-grade students were by checking your school's records. Now check for 1920. How many students moved away and how many new students joined the class in 1920. By using five-year intervals, you can get a good idea of the rate of mobility for earlier periods in your town's history. Now you can supply a local answer to the question, Is America still on the move?

25

ON THE MOVE–
PART II

Having developed a rate-of-mobility table (see On the Move, Part I), you might want to find out where people are moving to and from.

Prepare a map that notes the places you have lived since you were born or since the first grade. Then choose some subjects from your first-grade class picture and find out where they moved to when they left your class. Did they remain in the area or did they move a great distance away? Do the same thing for people who have joined your class. Where did they come from? School records often have this kind of information.

If you can, compare your generation's mobility with earlier times. School records dating as far back as 1905 or even 1885, for example, might indicate the towns from which new students moved.

Now you can ask some new questions. Do the people leaving your town today move to the same kind of town? How about those moving in? How does this compare with earlier times? Are people moving greater distances than they did in the early 1900's? You might compare your impressions with your grandparents' or with a town historian's.

You can present your findings in several ways. Use different colored pins on your map, such as blue for the towns people moved to, and red for the towns people moved from. If you compare years, you can use yellow and green for 1930, for instance, and orange and black for 1900. When you have all the pins arranged, do you see any patterns emerging? Can you think of any historical events or trends that might explain these patterns? During what periods has your town had its greatest growth? How does the future of your town look?

26

HEROES AND CULTURE

Sometimes a lot can be learned about a country by examining its culture heroes, those well-known personalities who are generally liked or respected. But as time passes, culture heroes change, and these changes often are a good indication of shifts in a nation's style and values.

This project suggests some ways of identifying America's culture heroes. To make things easier, we suggest that you do not include politicians in your list of candidates. Not because politicians aren't liked, respected or worthy of hero worship, but because people's feelings about politicians change so quickly that they are not a very reliable indication of national trends.

One approach is to look at past and present TV programming. Check *The New York Times* index in your local library for Nielsen ratings. Who was popular on TV five years ago, for instance? What types of programs did people like best? In the early 1960's, nearly every network had a show about doctors. Does any one theme seem to be popular now? What seems to be the appeal of the current TV stars?

Another possibility is to check the covers of the major weekly magazines. Magazine editors often select attention-getting faces so that the public will want to read what's inside. If the cover personality is not a politician, government official or someone involved in a "hot" news item, he or she may well be a culture

hero. Try writing to the public relations departments of several of the major magazines. Ask them which cover personalities produced the best newsstand sales. Does David Cassidy outdraw Wilt Chamberlain? Does he outdraw the Rolling Stones?

From all this information you can begin to focus on some conclusions. Consider the following questions for ideas:

(1) What areas seem to produce the most heroes—sports, entertainment, science, law, government, arts?

(2) To what extent do culture heroes seem to be created by the media?

(3) Who are your heroes? Why?

(4) Why do we have culture heroes?

(5) Why do culture heroes change? Do cowboy culture heroes appeal to kids anymore?

Survey students in your class to determine their heroes. Ask them to name people or offer a list of names and ask them to pick the person they most respect. You might also ask what magazines and books they read, what TV programs they watch and what records and radio programs they listen to. Does there seem to be any relationship between the things they read and

71

watch and listen to and the people they respect? Ask the same questions of the same people again in six months. Have their answers changed? Does the media seem to be responsible?

You can also find out a lot by using pictures. Get permission to hang pictures of culture heroes in your school cafeteria. The first day put up one picture. The second day put up another picture. How many people stop and look? How long do they look at each picture? Do the teachers seem to respond differently from the students? What about girls as compared to boys? Older students? Younger students? You might try the same experiment in a supermarket or a post office, but be sure to get permission first.

27

GOVERNMENT IN ACTION—PART I

Many people think of government as a group of men chosen to do a job. If we like the job they do, we re-elect them. If we don't, we elect someone else.

Actually a big part of an *elected* official's job is to see that the *appointed* officials do what they are being paid for. If the public wants a road from point A to point B, it's the elected official's job to see that the highway commission builds the road from A to B, not from B to C. Making government work can be very complicated, and understanding how it works can be even more complicated. In the three parts of this project (which can be done together or independently) we will be observing how government operates.

73

First, let's examine a local problem. Certainly there must be something in your town that needs fixing or correcting. Perhaps weeds are covering a stop sign or a bulb in a traffic light is burned out. Maybe a sidewalk or street is in serious need of repair or the playground needs a policeman at certain hours. How can you correct these problems?

You could pull up the weeds yourself. But changing the bulb in the traffic light is more difficult. And repairing the street is completely out of the question for a private citizen. Here you need action by your city, town or county government administrators. You don't need a law. You need service, and the task is to find out who to call, write or visit.

Use the telephone directory, which lists the various government departments serving your town. Call the department that seems most likely to handle your problem. Be prepared to describe the situation and its location. Write down the name of the person to whom you are speaking. After you hang up, jot down the answer you were given. What did he (she) say he (she) would do about the problem? He (she) may have advised you to call someone else. If so, repeat the above steps.

Now follow up. Was the problem solved? Who took care of it and when? (If you're lucky you may even see the repairs taking place. If so, ask the repairmen how they learned about the job to be done. Do they have to write a report when the work is completed? Out of courtesy you might explain why you're asking these questions.) If nothing happens, call the government department again and ask to speak to the person who handled your original request.

If it's practical, you might also visit the person you talked with on the phone. Explain who you are and ask what action he (she) took. Did he (she) call someone? Leave a note? Write a letter? Who actually ordered the repair work?

74 At the end of this project you should have a list of the dates, times and names of people you called and the actions taken to solve the problem. Probably you will find that several telephone operators, secretaries, supervisors and repairmen were involved. Somewhere in the office files there may be a form describing the problem, with your name as the citizen who re-

ported it. But regardless, you will have learned something about how government works at the local level.

If you can't get any action or aren't given a good reason why you should forget the whole thing, what can you do? Does it seem reasonable to contact an elected official and explain the difficulties you've had getting service? Would it seem sensible to call a local newspaper and find out what they know about getting government service?

28

GOVERNMENT IN ACTION—PART II

The problems described in Part I of this project are administrative and are anticipated by governments. In fact, money is set aside for such things as street repairs, extra police patrols, etc.

Now let's look into the law-making process of local government. When a government enacts a law, it changes something or introduces something new. Perhaps the law alters the tax structure or authorizes the building of a new road or lowers the legal driving age. In any case, it's one thing to report a bad pothole on Maple Street. It's another thing to call and say, "Please build a new road off Main Street."

Start by looking up the agenda for the next meeting of your local government. If you can't find it in the local newspaper, call the town hall and ask for a copy.

From the agenda, select a legislative proposal that seems interesting. Then research the background for this proposal. Your best sources, unless your parents are acquainted with the issue, are local newspapers and the town clerk. Visit both and ask if they can explain what this proposal is all about. Who first asked for the new law to be passed? How long has the proposal been under discussion? Was a group appointed to study the matter? Who favors the proposal? Who is against it? What would change if the proposal becomes law? Will these changes cost anything? How much?

Keep a record of all the answers to these questions. If the bill involves a big issue, the local radio station may have information. Newspapers may be running editorials and letters to the editor on the subject.

You might also wish to visit the person who first proposed the bill. How did he proceed? Did he call someone? Did he get a member of government to make the proposal for him? How long has he been working on this proposal? If an elected official first thought of the proposal, where did he get his idea?

If the proposal is controversial, you will probably find that legislative action takes much longer than the administrative action described in Part I. Your folder of newspaper clippings and notes of what people have told you should give you a very interesting and clear record of how an idea becomes law.

77

29

GOVERNMENT IN ACTION—PART III

What is the role of the police and the courts in local government? To fully understand courtroom and legal procedures, you must be a lawyer or have a great deal of legal and courtroom experience. Watching a TV program or a movie that shows a courtroom in action can be very misleading.

One way you can begin to understand legal procedure is to study the life of a speeding ticket from the time it is given to the speeder by the policeman to the time the speeder either pays his fine or is judged innocent. In most states, a speeder must go to court, although some states permit payment by mail. Since speeding cases are among the most common cases brought to court, it would be useful to understand the procedure and people involved.

Your best sources are a policeman and a clerk or secretary at your town, city or county court. A local lawyer might be able to fill you in on many of the details. The policeman can tell what his responsibility is. To whom does he send the citation for speeding? How is the information entered on the court records? What choices does an accused speeder have? If he does not believe he is guilty, what can he do? Here you may find that the policeman, lawyer and the local judge can offer some interesting information. If the accused speeder admits he is guilty, what must he do? How is his punishment decided?

What are the choices for the speeder who thinks the punishment is unfair? When the fine is paid, where does the money go? Is a record of the case kept? Where? When we say that some-one has a criminal record, what does that mean?

You can learn something about local courts by following other cases involving a littering violation, an arrest for shop-lifting or destruction of property or even more serious crimes. A lawyer or a policeman can explain some of the procedural differences between various crimes and the differences in treat-ment of adults and minors.

And by all means watch the court in action. Many cities hold night court, which is open to the public. Or ask your teacher to organize a field trip to the courthouse, preferably when an interesting case is on the docket. It can be fascinating. The courts are an important part of government in action, and study-ing something as simple as a traffic-violation ticket can help you understand how our courts work.

30

WEIGHTS AND MEASURES

A man drives into a gas station, reaches into the back seat or trunk of his car and gets out a small pail. He says to the attendant, "One gallon, please." When the pail is filled to a certain line, the reading on the pump had better be exactly one gallon. If it is less, the gas-station operator or owner could be fined or arrested, for the man with the pail is an inspector of weights and measures.

Why do we need inspectors of weights and measures? Stories are often told about the fat butcher who pressed his stomach against the scales when he was weighing meat, so the customer paid for something he didn't get—a portion of the butcher's stomach. Or the dry-goods dealer with broad thumbs, who cheated the public when measuring material with a yardstick, because he included his thumbs in the measurement.

Today, however, when many items, such as gasoline, are measured by machines, sometimes a faulty machine is responsible for a short measure. So the federal, state, county or town government (or all four) appoint inspectors to protect the public from mechanical or human error or dishonest people.

When our gas "customer" (with the pail) finishes checking all the pumps in the gas station, he'll place a small, colored seal on each pump:

Inspected and approved
(date)
(signature)
Inspector of Weights and Measures

Find out who the inspector of weights and measures is in your community. Ask if you can accompany him on his rounds. Get information about:

    (1) His training
        a) What special skills are necessary for the job?
        b) How long did it take him to prepare for the job?
        c) How did he get the job—through examination or appointment?
    (2) What he inspects
        a) gasoline pumps?
        b) scales in stores?
        c) scales at sand and gravel pits, coal yards?
        d) meters on oil trucks?
        e) materials dispensers at dry-goods stores?
        f) soft-drink machines?
        g) rope or electric-cable dispensers?
    (3) Frequency of his inspections
    (4) What he does when he finds short or long measures
    (5) How people react to him

Your project could be entitled simply "A Day with the Inspector of Weights and Measures." Follow-ups could include other public officials. Perhaps the mayor, police chief, sanitation commissioner or building inspector would be happy to have you study his job for a day.

31

THE CEMETERY

There's a lot to be learned from a cemetery. The purpose of this project is to see what you can discover about your town's history by studying a local cemetery.

First, who owns the cemetery? Was it originally a family burial ground? Who cared for it? Who maintains it now?

Observe the last names of the people buried there. Do the names seem to reflect a particular ethnic background? Does the start of the cemetery (as indicated by the earliest dates on headstones) coincide with the migration of a particular group of people into your area?

What were the ages of the people buried there? Did older generations live shorter lives than more recent generations? Did men live longer than women? What about infant or child mortality? Did childhood diseases result in more deaths in the past than they do today? Can you see any evidence that some mothers died in childbirth? A comparison of family births and deaths will give you some clues.

You might want to write down the names of many people buried in the cemetery, together with dates of their birth and death, and then verify your analysis by referring to books on local history and newspapers of the period. Notice if many deaths occurred in a particular year. This might indicate an epidemic or natural disaster that is part of your town's history.

32

GARBAGE—PART I

Today the average Swede produces two and two-tenths pounds of garbage a day. How much does the average American produce? You can begin to find the answer to this question by keeping track of your family's garbage.

You'll need a scale—perhaps a spring balance—some strong plastic bags and, on occasion, a strong stomach. Weighing the total amount of garbage each week is not much of a problem, but sorting and classifying it might be.

Start by having the garbage presorted. Ask your family to use one plastic bag for all paper, another for metal cans, and still another for "live" garbage such as cooking waste, potato peels, apple cores, etc.

To analyze the proportion of garbage that is biodegradable —that will rot—keep a separate bag for all plastic containers, aluminum foil, aluminum cans, plastic wrap, etc.

In addition to finding the weight and classifying the garbage, you might also want to determine the number of cubic feet of garbage your family creates each week. Get a container that has a known volume or build a box, say, one foot high, one foot wide and one foot long. That's one cubic foot. Now pack your family's garbage into the box. The total number of boxes you fill equals the volume. If you fill three boxes, your family produced three cubic feet of garbage that week.

Actually volume may be a more important measure than weight, since many towns compress garbage and use it for landfill. So the volume of land that your family could fill each week is directly proportional to the volume of garbage produced.

Try to enlist a number of people to carry out this project to see if your family is "average" in your area. Once you've gathered your data, your school or the town council might be interested in your findings, particularly if they are planning a campaign to call attention to the problems of garbage collection.

You might also ask yourself some questions. How do you feel about the amount of garbage your family produces? Can you think of ways to cut down the quantity or to eliminate certain kinds of garbage? Do you think garbage is something private citizens should worry about?

33

GARBAGE—PART II

Some people say you can find out a lot of useful information about a neighborhood or individual family by examining its garbage. For example, if the garbage contains generous amounts of fresh fruit leftovers, such as banana peels, orange skins, melon rinds, etc., during the winter months in a cold climate, that family or neighborhood probably has a fair amount of money. Less affluent people would not be buying high-priced fresh fruit in the winter.

The purpose of this project is to decide whether analyzing garbage provides useful information. It might be a difficult project to carry out, but for an enterprising (or lucky) student the results could be revealing.

Figure out some way to get garbage from an affluent area and from a poor area. Maybe you know someone who owns a garbage-collecting service or perhaps you know some people who wouldn't mind your rummaging around in their garbage.

When you get the garbage samples look for the following: From the wealthy area—

(1) Cans of expensive brands of food that come from gourmet shops.
(2) Bones from expensive cuts of meat, such as sirloin steak, loin lamb chops, rib roast, etc.
(3) Boxes from exclusive clothing stores or sports shops in your town.
(4) Containers from expensive types of seafood such as lobster, shrimp, crab, etc.
(5) Magazines and newspapers. What can you tell from the reading material?

From the poor area—

(1) Cans with supermarket labels from A & P, Safeway, Shoprite, Grand Union, First National, etc.
(2) Bones from less expensive cuts of meat such as stew bones, chuck roasts, etc. If you don't find many bones at all, it may indicate that the family has a dog or that they eat a lot of boneless meat such as hamburger and hot dogs or that they are vegetarians.

87

    (3) Bags and boxes from local discount stores.
    (4) Containers from relatively inexpensive items such as spaghetti, economy bags from frozen vegetables, etc.

It's important not to overgeneralize about your findings. Families with young children, for example, might buy a lot of hot dogs simply because the kids like hot dogs. If you can follow up with personal interviews with the families, so much the better. It might also be interesting to list the contents of the two kinds of garbage and then ask your classmates what they think they can deduce about the families. Be sure to keep the names of the families involved confidential.

34

HABITS

Are you a predictable person? Do you have definite habits and routines? In this project we are suggesting that you explore your unconscious habits.

For example, consider the following questions:

    (1) In a particular class, do you sit in the same seat every day? Why?

    (2) Do you try to sit in a similar place in every classroom—in the front row, rear row, nearest to the door or window or teacher's desk?

    (3) Do you sit at the same lunch table during lunch?

    (4) At home, do you use the same chair at mealtimes? Do you sit or lie in the same place to watch TV or read a book? Are special chairs reserved for your mother and father? Why?

Most people have habits and patterns that they are not really aware of. Think about your own, and you'll be ready to observe or question others about their habits. Your teachers, for instance, probably have certain patterns they follow in the classroom. Your baby brother may have already begun to develop patterns. Does your father read his newspaper at a certain time, in a certain place, in a certain way? When shopping for groceries, does your mom or dad follow a certain pattern in the store—milk first, then meat, etc.?

You can discover some interesting things about yourself and others by attempting to understand habits. Next to each habit you've identified, jot down an explanation or the words "no reason." If you can, get others to try your study on themselves, and compare answers. How many "no reasons" do you have? If you came up with a reason such as "I like Sally and she always sits there," that's not really a reason, unless Sally has a good reason for sitting there!

The point of this study is not to show that you have to have a specific reason for everything you do. It is to illustrate that people develop habits for a variety of reasons. The foremost one seems to be that patterns can make life easier. But they can also get in the way. It might be fun to try to figure out which patterns help you and which slow you down or make you less flexible. How do you think you acquired your habits? Did you learn them from others? Or did you invent them all by yourself?

35

RHYTHMS

Have you ever complained that your life is dull, that the same old things happen every day? You get up in the morning, go to the bathroom, bathe, eat breakfast, get on a bus or subway or walk to school. Then you have classes, eat lunch, have more classes, walk or ride home, have a couple of hours to work or play, eat supper, do homework and go to bed.

This sequence of events could be called a rhythm, or pattern, of your life. This type of rhythm is defined in the dictionary as "movement or fluctuation marked by the regular recurrence or natural flow of related elements."

All of us live according to a certain flow of related elements. The broadest of these natural elements is life itself; we are born, we live and we die. Another broad element common to all of us is the seasons. Another is digestion; you eat, your body processes the food, then you get rid of the waste products.

Go out on a city street at the time when people are going to work. You are likely to see streets jammed with cars and sidewalks crowded with people. Go out again at midnight and you will see deserted streets and empty sidewalks.

Stand on the same corner or watch carefully from your school-bus window and you'll probably see the same people going to work, getting their newspapers, walking the dog, etc.

The object of this project is to recognize these patterns. Make a list of them, organized in some logical manner. For example, three major headings might be:

> Rhythms people don't control
> Rhythms people control that affect me
> Rhythms I control

(1) Rhythms people don't control:
    a) being born, living, dying (*time* of death can be controlled)
    b) the turning earth
       1) seasons
       2) hours of daylight and darkness
       3) tides
    c) bodily functions
       1) heartbeat and circulation
       2) growth of cells
       3) digestion (somewhat controlled)
       4) need for activity
       5) need for sleep
    d) _____

(2) Rhythms people control that affect me:
    a) time to get up (to some extent)
    b) time for school to start
    c) class schedules
    d) time to eat and what and how much I eat (to some extent)
    e) _____

(3) Rhythms I control:
    a) time to get up (to some extent)
    b) bathing
    c) watching television
    d) doing homework
    e) how I feel
       1) moods (to some extent)
       2) how I react to people (to some extent)
    f) _____

Weekly and monthly rhythms are important too: when report cards are due, when you get paid for a job or get your allowance, when your parents' rent, mortgage or car payment is due. Other more subtle rhythms might be noted. How often is your house or apartment painted? How frequently does the roof need to be replaced? How long does an automobile last?

The recognition of rhythms shows you what you have in common with all people and helps you to identify parts of your day that might benefit from a little more variety.

36

PRESSURE

Concern with time often leads to pressure. All of us have to get assignments in on time, and most of us wait until the last minute to start working on them. Working against time, we tend to feel a sense of urgency, or pressure. We worry that things won't get done, we stay up late and we constantly look at the clock. Even the word "deadline" seems ominous.

We feel the same time pressure when watching games. We get anxious, particularly if the score is fairly even. We tend to watch the clock, wishing to hold back the hands when our team is behind and hoping time would hurry up the clock when they're ahead.

There are many other kinds of pressure. There is the pressure to do better than someone else in sports or schoolwork. There is the pressure you feel when you and your best friend have an argument or when everything seems to be going wrong.

The purpose of this project is to study pressure—what causes it and how you and others react to it. You might start by keeping two records. On one, list the events that make you feel pressured. On the other, list your reactions to pressure: do you cry, kick the door, yell at your mother, become very calm? What do you do? If you can, compare your pulse rate during times of pressure and times of relaxation. Which events produce the fastest pulse? You might also note what others do under pressure. How does your mother react when your brothers and sisters are screaming for dinner? Do you blame her?

Studying the lists you've made will help you to better understand yourself and your family and friends.

37

HORSEPOWER

Not long ago a newspaper in a large eastern city carried a picture of an old bony horse drawing a junk wagon, captioned "The Last Horse." It was the last horse existing in that city. But today there are fifteen horses housed within that city's limits. Interestingly, none of these new horses are used to pull wagons nor do they do any other work for man. They are there to be ridden for sport by their owners.

Today, when virtually no horses are used as beasts of burden, there are about 15,000,000 horses in the United States, an increase of 100 percent since 1940. The period since 1940 also marks extensive use of farm machinery. One would think that an increased use of tractors, etc., would cut down on the horse population.

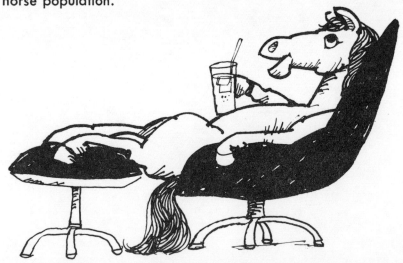

The small state of Connecticut, mainly an industrial and business state, has 7.3 horses per square mile, more than any other state in the nation. In just ten years the state's horse population has increased from 20,000 to its present 30,000. What does the increase in horse population mean to an area's economy? What does it mean to you, a horse lover?

The suggestion for this project is to gather all of the information you can about horse population. Your town or city clerk can give you an idea of how many horses there are in your area. More accurately, he can tell you the number of horses that taxes were paid on. (Some people who own horses don't pay the taxes.)

Through town records try to determine:

(1) the town horse population
    a) now
    b) five years ago
    c) ten years ago
    d) twenty-five years ago
(2) the uses of the horses during the various periods
(3) the estimated value of the horses
(4) reasons for increases and decreases in horse population during a specific period

You might also want to consider how much business horse ownership generates for the community. For example, it is estimated that the 30,000 horses in Connecticut provide jobs for 1,000 people involved with racing and riding stables, and produce more than $3,000,000 in revenue annually. You can get an idea of how much it costs to maintain a horse in your area by interviewing a few people who own horses.

How much does it cost for:

    (1) feed
        a) hay
        b) grain

(2) care
  a) shoeing
  b) veterinarians' fees
  c) medicines
  d) supplies
  e) board (if any)
(3) equipment
  a) tack—saddles, bridles, etc.
  b) fences, etc.

If you've been trying to persuade your dad to get you a horse, you'd better do this survey *after* you get it. If your father sees the figures before, you'll probably never ride a horse of your own.

38

YEAR-ROUND SCHOOL?

Many school planners and experts believe that year-round schools will be functioning within the next five to ten years. In fact, you already may have an extended school year program (ESY) to look forward to. The goal of the ESY programs is to get more use out of school facilities (buildings, equipment, etc.) for less money.

You might find out what plans, if any, are being made by your town to extend the school year through the summer months. But you should also know that most ESY programs may not *require* students to go to school in the summer. Various plans are in operation: a 45-15 plan in which students go to school 45 days and are off 15; a plan whereby children can attend school in the summer if they wish and advance one quarter of a school year each summer; a plan in which students can go to school any three quarters each year and take one quarter vacation time.

The information you need will have to be collected from the people who make decisions regarding education—that board of education and its chief executive, the superintendent of schools. School principals, teachers, parents and students might also be consulted to find out what their attitudes are toward an ESY plan.

Once you gather some information, you might want to sample public opinion. Write up a brief paragraph describing each program, including the present program of your school. Ask each person to rate each program and ask for comments and questions about each proposal.

You can also get additional information from the people you interview. If they are adults, do they have children in school, what is the father's and the mother's occupation, educational background, age? If they are students, what is their grade?

With background on ESY as well as information from your survey, you may want to present your findings to a member of the board of education or to the P-TA. And if you attend a P-TA meeting, you may get a chance to hear audience reaction to ESY. Be sure you compare the reactions at the meeting to comments on your survey. Are they as well thought out as the written answers? How do you feel about ESY?

39

HAIR

How long do you wear your hair? A funny answer might be: Until it falls out. But to many people the question of hair styles is no laughing matter. Hair has caused controversy among children, parents, teachers and school administrators. And the controversy goes far beyond what you and your parents may think about your individual hair style.

For example, university placement officers are advising seniors that shoulder-length hair and unkempt beards can be obstacles when job hunting. According to surveys, placement personnel say, many employers still prefer shaved faces and short hair.

SOCIAL SCIENCE PROJECTS YOU CAN DO

One of the authors of this book has a beard. A waitress in a place where he often eats said to him, "You used to be such a nice man until you grew that beard." Why had her attitude toward him changed because of the hair on his face?

However, there is also evidence that negative attitudes toward beards, long hair and "weirdo" hair styles are changing. In the armed forces, professional sports and in many businesses, long hair is tolerated—sometimes even celebrated.

How do people who live in your area feel about hair?

Draw up a list of the names of people in various occupations and age ranges that you might survey in person or by questionnaire.

This list might include: employers (personnel managers of large companies); people in federal and local government agencies such as postmen, policemen and firemen; public school personnel such as superintendents, assistant superintendents, principals and teachers. Be sure to include some private citizens, because the feelings of private citizens are often a reflection of (or stimulus for) the policies of large organizations.

Poll local storekeepers, bank managers, barbers, clergymen, students and parents and grandparents of friends with questions such as:

    (1) How do you feel about men wearing shoulder-length hair?

    (2) Would you hire a man who had long hair, a beard, a moustache?

    (3) Why do you like or dislike long hair, beards?

Another approach might be to obtain "before" and "after" pictures of someone who now wears a beard and long hair; or two pictures, one of a long-haired bearded individual and another of a clean-shaven person.

Present the pictures to your respondents and ask who they would hire, stop to help on the highway or buy something from in a store. Be sure to ask why. Keep track of the age range, sex and job classification of the respondents. You might even try to find out what political party they belong to. Your findings should be interesting.

(1) Who won your poll—hair or clean-shaven?
(2) What reasons were given for choosing one over the other?
(3) Did age, sex or job seem to determine how a person answered?
(4) Did political party affiliation seem to have any bearing on how a person reacted to your questions?

Some final questions: How do you wear your hair? Why?

40

MASS PRODUCTION

Charles Kettering astounded the automotive world in 1909 by disassembling three identical Cadillac automobiles, mixing the parts in a pile and then reassembling three complete automobiles. Of course, he was demonstrating one of the principles of mass production—the interchangeability of parts.

The most commonly known principle of mass production is the assembly line, where parts move along a conveyor belt and each employee attaches a part such as a wheel, or a door, on a partially completed automobile. Each employee becomes expert at performing his specific function and, in theory, he can do the job better and faster because he repeats the operation over and over. But before the assembly-line employees can do their jobs, someone has to figure out the order in which the parts should be put together. Someone has to set up the assembly line.

This project suggests that you set up a simple mass-production operation. Figure out how to mass produce something like wooden wall candleholders or bookends.

Wall candleholder:

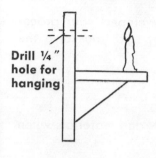

Drill ¼" hole for hanging

Back of Candle Holder, approximately 3" x 8"

Candle Platform, approximately 2" x 2½"

Triangular Platform Support

Driil halfway through candle platform to make mounting hole for candle. Use a drill bit that is the same diameter as the candle.

You will need a small supply of ½" or ⅜" plywood, some finishing nails (¾" to 1"), stain or paint, sandpaper, glue and stiff cardboard.

Your tools would be: saw, hammer, drill, paintbrush.

Out of the cardboard, make a pattern of each part. Then, while timing yourself, cut out each part and assemble one complete candleholder.

Now, using your patterns, cut out several of the same parts —perhaps eight—then assemble all eight candleholders. Be sure to time yourself while assembling these, too.

Some questions:

(1) How long did it take you to assemble each candleholder? Did you follow the same procedure for each holder?

(2) Are all eight candleholders of the same quality?

(3) Do the parts fit well, that is, are they interchangeable?

(4) Would your system be more efficient if you made some jigs or tools to hold the parts as you worked on them? (For example, nailing the triangular piece from the back is rather difficult. Putting this against another triangular piece may make the job easier.)

105

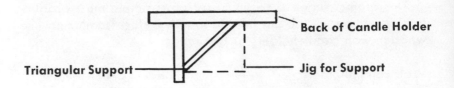

The steps that you followed as you developed your procedures would be of interest to others. How did you solve the problems of:

(1) interchangeability
(2) assembly sequence
(3) having a ready supply of parts and materials when and where needed

How and why did your efficiency increase (or decrease) in terms of:

(1) quality of the product
(2) time needed to make the product
(3) cost of materials

If you work this project right, perhaps you may be able to make some money from it—wall candleholders could be a big seller at Christmas time.

41

DIALECT STUDY:
VOCABULARY

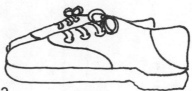

What do *you* call these objects?

Do you call them sneaks, sneakers, tennis shoes, gym shoes or something else? The name that you give to this form of footwear depends, in part, on where you live and how old you are.

Scientists called linguists can tell where people came from just by listening to the words they use to identify common objects. See what you can learn with this simple test.

Obtain pictures of many familiar objects such as the ones pictured below. (A large department store catalog is an excellent source.) Ask as many people as you can to identify each picture for you. In your sample, be sure to include people of your own age as well as older people.

After you find out what words people use for these objects, you will have to know something about the people. This sample questionnaire might be useful in getting started:

State_____ County_____ Town_____
How long have you lived here? _____
Birthplace _____
About how old are you? _____
Have you traveled much outside this state? _____

SOCIAL SCIENCE PROJECTS YOU CAN DO

The vocabulary that people use is influenced by many things, but at this point we are interested only in:

(1) vocabulary differences caused by differences in age
(2) vocabulary differences caused by differences in where people came from

To get started on this project you will need:

Questionnaire	Pictures to be Identified	Answer Sheet
State	1. ☐ 6. ☐	1. ___ 6. ___
County	2. ☐ 7. ☐	2. ___ 7. ___
Town	3. ☐ 8. ☐	3. ___ 8. ___
Etc.	4. ☐ 9. ☐	4. ___ 9. ___
	5. ☐ 10. ☐	5. ___ 10. ___

(One for Each Person)   (Just One to Be Used for All)   (One for Each Person)

Collect the information from as many people as possible. Now you're ready to make a display. Next to each picture, list the name you would give to the object. Then put down the names other people give the object.

Object	My Name for It	Other People's Names for It	Where Respondents Grew Up	Approximate Age of Respondents
	Pajamas	P.J.'s Sleepers Pajamas Dr. Denton's	_____ _____ _____ _____	_____ _____ _____ _____

From this survey, what conclusions can you draw about your town?

42

PROPAGANDA—
PART I

Have you noticed that at election time candidates often begin to mention all of the bad things their opponents have done? Or the candidates will have their pictures taken when they're shaking hands with people in stores, factories or on the farm? A politician usually is a pretty good master of the art of persuasion or propaganda—bringing a group of people around to his way of thinking.

Television commercials and newspaper and magazine advertisements also use several types of propaganda. Car manufacturer X, for example, might advertise his low-priced cars by trumpeting a long list of equipment such as two-speed windshield wipers, seat belts and emergency flashers. "All this," he might say, "for the low, low price of $2,200." What he doesn't tell you is that all cars, by law, must have this equipment.

This project asks you to identify the different kinds of propaganda seen in magazine or newspaper ads and TV commercials. We suggest that you look for propaganda that falls into the following categories (developed by Nila Banton Smith, and we think they are the best available):

(1) *Bad names and glad names*

Bad names encourage the consumer to judge the competitors' products without looking at the facts. An ad that says "our car rides smoother than a $10,000 limousine" implies that the $10,000 limousine isn't worth the money, which may be true, but the ad doesn't offer any facts to back up the claim. "Better than the high-priced spread" is another example of bad-name propaganda.

Glad-name ads use such words as charming, lovely, beautiful, highest grade, etc. These words don't tell you anything concrete about the product; they just say, "like it."

(2) *Transfer*

The idea of transfer is to have us think about something we like while we're thinking about a particular product. If a fabric softener is said to make your clothes "baby soft," then you think about babies. If you feel good about babies, you probably have good feelings about the product.

(3) *Testimonial*

This is one of the easiest forms of propaganda to spot. A famous personality says, "I like this product. I use it all the time and it's great." Because we like or respect the personality, we may try the product.

(4) *Bandwagon*

In parades, years ago, bands were carried on top of special horse-drawn wagons. Spectators often climbed on the bandwagon. Now, when a lot of people do the same thing (or are asked to do the same thing), the phrase "bandwagon" is applied. Have you even said to your parents, "But everyone else is going, why can't I?" This is bandwagon propaganda. Ads that say things like, "Nine out of ten people" or "millions of Americans" are using the bandwagon approach.

(5) *Plain folks*

Picture a happy family going to a drive-in restaurant for dinner. The restaurant is a family eating place, for plain folks like you and me. Because most of us consider ourselves to be average people, or plain folks, we may have good feelings about the product being advertised.

(6) *Stacking the cards*

110

Car manufacturer X, mentioned earlier, is stacking the cards. He's telling you a lot of "facts" and hoping that you'll think they are more special than they really are. One of the characteristics of this form of propaganda is half truths masquerading as whole truths.

Keep an eye out for ads that use several different types of propaganda at the same time. For instance, "Mr. Man-on-the-Street, I see you are wearing our new, longer lasting, better fitting, brightly colored, easy to wash and wear, cheap, durable tie. How do you like it?" This is definitely the *glad-name* approach combined with *plain folks*. And there's a little *stacking the cards* in there, too. What do you think?

43

PROPAGANDA—
PART II

This project asks you to identify the types of propaganda found in newspaper stories. A good time to do this project is during a political campaign. Consider the following headline: "Mayor calls opponent a liar"—obviously a *bad name*. A member of the mayor's staff refers to the mayor's diligence and honesty—obviously *glad names*.

The candidate and his family are pictured going to church. The assumption is that we, the public, like people who go to church, *so we will transfer* this good feeling to the candidate.

When the President campaigns for a particular candidate, the candidate is using the *testimonial* form of propaganda. Movie stars, too, are in politics, and in many instances their support will serve as a *testimonial* for their chosen candidates.

Listen to the candidates a few weeks before the election. Each claims that he is going to win. Each is trying to get the uncommitted voter, the citizen who hasn't yet made up his mind, to join his *bandwagon*.

The *plain folks* kind of propaganda is still very evident in politics. A candidate asks housewives about prices. He kisses babies. He judges livestock at a county fair. Why? He wants to show that what interests us, interests him. He wants to get the idea across that he's *plain folks* just like the rest of us, and if all of us *plain folks* get together we could elect him.

Naturally, candidates for election want only the best things about them publicized. This is normal. Each of us would like people to think only good things about us. But candidates may be *stacking the cards* if they tell us only the good things they have done and never mention the things that they failed to do.

Look for these forms of propaganda in other kinds of news items. What shape does propaganda take when a power company and a citizens' group have sharp conflicts about a pollution problem? Is propaganda involved when a policeman and a suspect argue about police brutality? One way of sorting through the news and making decisions about issues is to figure out what kind of propaganda you're dealing with.

For your project, you might list the categories of propaganda. Under each, include the news stories that seem to apply. Underline the key phrases, and be sure to watch for multiple forms of propaganda. When a movie star endorses a candidate, for instance, this may be both *testimonial* and *transfer*.

How effective do you think propaganda is? Do you think any of your current ideas and opinions have been influenced by successful propaganda? What about those of your family and friends? Do we really look at the facts when we form an opinion? Are the facts always available?

44

CHANGE IN A LIFETIME

History is often viewed as a series of dates. In 1903, the Wright brothers flew their plane for the first time. In 1969, the first man landed on the moon. But history often doesn't mean much to us when we view it by dates.

One way to give history meaning is to associate it with people you know. It's quite possible, for example, that your grandfather was alive when the Wright brothers took off and that he *saw* the first man walk on the moon. Your great-grandfather was probably alive when there were no automobiles and the telephone was a recent invention. He may have lived to see Charles Lindbergh fly across the Atlantic Ocean and cars travel at speeds of over fifty miles an hour.

History is more than dates. History is all about change. In some places and at some times, change occurs very slowly. In the United States, certainly in the twentieth century, changes have been very rapid. So rather than view change as a series of dates, relate it to a lifetime. Find out the dates your ancestors were born and died. Perhaps your great-grandfather lived from 1880 to 1930. His father might have lived from 1855 to 1910.

114

Now think about some of the major events of history. Your great-great-grandfather was probably alive during the Civil War. He might have left some letters. Or perhaps he told his children about some of his experiences and impressions, and they passed them on to your grandfather, who can tell you about them. What do you think your great-great-grandfather would have thought about Korea and Vietnam? Ask your grand-father and grandmother about some of the changes they've seen. How do they feel about these changes?

Once we see history as a series of lifetimes in which change occurred, we can understand better what the events meant to the people who lived through them. We can also begin to under-stand why some older people seem to resist change. After all, if you were born during World War I, lived through the De-pression, World War II, Korea and Vietnam; saw the influence of mass media, the change from farm to city living, the assassi-nations of John and Robert Kennedy and Martin Luther King, you, too, might wish that things would slow down a bit.

Even in your lifetime there have been many changes. Make a list of the important ones. Have they affected you? Is your school using the same history book that was used last year? Is your little sister learning to read by the same method you learned? Think about the changes you would like to see.

You can present the results of your research in several in-teresting ways. One way would be to draw a time-line of events, including the dates your ancestors were born and died. Then you can compare the rate of change in recent times with times in the past. You can also demonstrate change with pic-tures. Using twenty-year intervals, compare some of the typical scenes viewed by you, your parents, your grandparents and great-grandparents. In which twenty-year periods have the big-gest visual changes occurred?

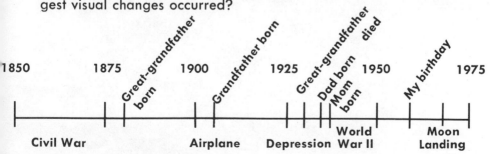

45

ANIMAL BEHAVIOR

If you live on a farm or have an opportunity to observe animals, you might be interested in a study of animal behavior.

In a visit to a chicken coop (or sheep pen or cow barn, etc.) you've probably noticed that the whole flock or herd of animals behaves in a certain way. But, as with people who share behavior patterns, the individuals in the group also behave in individual ways.

Catch a rooster and a hen and mark their tail feathers with colored chalk or a felt-tip marker. Tying a piece of colored

yarn around each chicken's leg is also a good means of identification. Then spend some time charting their behavior within the flock. You might be interested in:

(1) How they react to noises—normal sounds and the special sounds you make.

(2) Their physical movements. How far do they travel in the course of a few hours or in a day?

(3) Their eating and drinking habits. How often do they eat? If they have a choice do they always eat and drink from the same feeder?

(4) Their nesting and roosting habits. Does the hen use the same nest each day? Does the rooster have a predictable number of sex contacts during a period of time?

(5) How do the animals react to daylight and darkness? When do they begin to roost? What role does the rooster seem to play during twilight hours?

(6) The sounds they make. When the hen clucks, is she responding to some other sound? When the rooster crows, does he seem to be signalling something?

Now, if possible, isolate the animals you have studied. Be sure to keep the solitary environment as similar to the group environment as possible. Keep detailed records of each animal's behavior in isolation. What can you observe?

Chickens make good subjects, but you can observe horses (especially colts), kittens or puppies. The main point of your project is to determine how individuals behave within a larger group of animals. What can be considered group-induced behavior? What is clearly individual behavior?

46

THE NUMBERS GAME—
PART I

A friend recently opened his wallet and exclaimed, "Good grief, I'm literally numbed by numbers!" Here's what he found:

041-26-4747—Social Security number

885-650-912-0—gasoline company credit card number

726-729-942-16—gasoline company credit card number

3-80565-98798-5—department store credit card number

009-396-f24-07—automobile insurance policy number

022418393—driver's license number

5760123252—automobile identification number

PRO170593—job identification number

06250—Zip code number

51152801—former army service number

The interesting thing about each of these numbers is that it is used in some way to identify something about the owner. In addition, these numbers seem to be more important to some people than his name. (Most of the identifying cards put the number first and name second.)

To find out more about numbers, investigate one that you will carry with you all your life. Go to your nearest Social Security office and apply for your Social Security number. You can get this number at any time, even if you don't have a job. But don't just get the number—find out what it means. What does each grouping of numbers stand for? How is a Social Security number usually used? Why do you have one in the first place? If your father or mother wanted to cash a check in a place where they weren't known, could they use their Social Security card as identification?

47

THE NUMBERS GAME–
PART II

Not too long ago, a soup company announced that it was recalling all cans of chicken vegetable soup packed by a particular plant, because of possible botulism contamination. The company gave the code number printed on the cans and urged consumers to destroy the soup and send in the label for a refund.

One of the authors of this book examined a can of chicken rice soup. Stamped on the metal top of the can was the number 05,P8X5B,5MI. On the label were several numbers including 10½ (oz.)—298 (grams). On the reverse side of the label were 1051-1 and 234567890ND17 0. What do all these numbers mean?

Now let's switch to automobiles. The automobile identification number of a friend (see The Numbers Game—Part I) is 5760123252. This indicates that it is a 1957 car, model 60 (if you know your cars, you'll recognize model 60 as a Cadillac) and it was the 123,252 car manufactured that year. Where was the car made? To whom was it first sold? All this information is also available through numbers.

This project suggests that you determine what information is available through numbers to the consumer when he buys items such as groceries, automobile tires, appliances, etc.

Select a product—corn flakes, for example. Write down all the mysterious numbers you can find on the box, then write to the manufacturer's public relations department to find out what the numbers mean.

For a car, you might talk to the service manager of a new car dealer. Talk to appliance dealers, supermarket managers or anybody who would know about the meaning and use of code numbers. These people are likely to have numbering systems themselves, and they might be happy to fill you in on some interesting details.

48

REPORTING THE
NEWS

We often hear it said that newspapers print the facts on the front page and opinion on the editorial page.

One way to test the truth of this assumption is to examine how different newspapers handle the same story. Start by comparing front pages. The front page, being the page everyone sees first, would seem to indicate how a newspaper feels about the importance of a story. Does one paper seem to consider a local strike more important than a presidential statement? Where does a certain front-page story appear? At the top right-hand column in one newspaper and down in the left-hand corner in another? Does the news story you're interested in appear on the front page of every newspaper you examine? What does the placement of a story tell you about the politics or readership of a newspaper?

Now, what are the headlines? One might read, "38 Radicals Bagged by Police," while another headline reporting the same event might say, "9 Hurt, 38 Arrested in Student Clash with Police." What do the different headline treatments seem to indicate?

Next, compare the reporting. Do all the papers report all the facts? Or do some facts appear in one paper, while a different selection of facts appears in another? If you put together the coverage in a variety of newspapers, do you think you'd have all the facts on a particular story?

Compare the pictures that accompany the story. Do they make you feel a certain way about the people or events described?

Compare the average length of news stories in various papers. Are articles generally longer in one paper than in another? Does the extra length usually mean that you're getting more facts? Does the length of a particular story seem to reflect how the newspaper feels about long or short stories? Or does it seem to indicate how the paper feels about *that* story?

Now summarize your research. Is the coverage pretty much the same? If each newspaper is saying the same thing about a particular event, check first to see that all the stories are not written by the same person or news service, such as Associated Press (AP) or United Press International (UPI). Local and regional papers can't afford to have reporters based all over the world, so they buy many stories from news services. If the coverage is different, try to explain why.

In your study you may want to include a comparison of different kinds of stories. Perhaps newspapers differ in their approach to some topics but not to others. In this instance, check the editorial pages to see if the opinions expressed there seem to explain the difference you observe in the news stories.

You can display your findings in two possible approaches:

First, arrange several newspaper articles on the same subject side by side. Underline the facts in one color and the editorial words and phrases, such as "major event," "tragedy," etc., in another color. This will give your viewers an opportunity to see the similarities and differences between various newspapers.

Second, exhibit the front pages for a certain day of several newspapers. Then indicate by arrows and short comments what you've learned about the meaning of a story's placement, the kind of headline it carries, the size of type used for the headline, the pictures and the relative lengths of the articles.

123

49

HISTORY THROUGH
STREET NAMES

Tommy Schultz lives on Cedar Avenue. But there aren't any cedar trees on Cedar Avenue. Does this mean that there were at one time? That a public official mistook an elm for a cedar? That the town once had a mayor named Cedar? How did Cedar Avenue get its name? The purpose of this project is to learn about your town by studying the names of schools, parks, streets and public buildings.

You will need a town or city map, as well as access to town records. The chances are that your town has a Main Street. But it may not always have been called Main Street, and it may not always have been *the* main street.

Early issues of a town newspaper might give you clues as to how street names have changed over the years. Town records may establish whether Green Street was named after Mr. Green or for the trees and shrubs that are (or were) on the street. How are street names decided? Who selected the names of streets in your town's residential areas? You might talk to a builder and find out what he knows about this process.

If the streets are numbered, find out the logic to the numbering system. In New York City, for example, why is First Avenue called First Avenue? Was it built first? Was it the first avenue in from the East River at one time? And who decided that it should be called First Avenue anyway?

Are your schools named for the streets they are on? For distinguished or prominent people? Are they numbered? Check with the board of education to find out how a school's name or number is decided. When did this custom for naming or numbering begin? Why was the practice adopted?

If your streets are named after important people, look up some information about them. Why did your town choose to honor them in this way? You may even want to propose a few names yourself if a new street is being built. You can learn the correct procedure from the town clerk.

To summarize and present your findings, you might start with a map and color code the streets. Use one color for typical names and numbers such as Main Street, Broad Street and Second Avenue. Use another color for streets named after national historical figures such as Washington or Kennedy. A third color could represent figures in local history. And a fourth color could indicate builders' decisions. From such a display, you can begin to generalize about your town's interest in its own local history or in national events, or both.

50

TOWN OR CITY GROWTH

As long as you are using town maps, explore the changes in your town since its earliest years. You should be able to see when each area was settled and to explain the reasons for whatever growth and change have taken place.

Your state or local historical association can be very helpful in this project. It often has a fine selection of old town maps and pictures. You may be able to find snapshots of some homes and stores that are still standing.

Many older homes have cornerstones, which mark the date when construction began. If you find that quite a number of buildings in a particular area were constructed at approximately the same time, remember that fires were frequent in the nineteenth century. Did this area replace an older, burned-out district?

Examine the residential areas as well as the business and industrial districts. From the town maps you can learn what sections remained woods or fields or swamp the longest. When did building start in these areas? Why? How were the building sites chosen? To face a road or a particular view? Did the streetcar or bus lines in your town influence where people built their homes and businesses? When did the railroad come to your town? Were a lot of businesses built after that date?

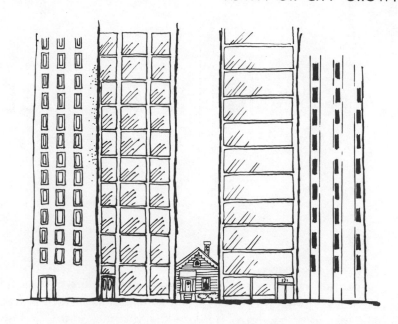

Is there a superhighway nearby with an exit for your town? Has this caused building and change? Are the newest buildings replacing the oldest buildings? Is the business area expanding and taking over formerly residential areas? Have new business areas, such as shopping centers, sprung up?

You can display your findings in several ways. You might use colors to indicate the age of buildings. For example, red for buildings older than 1850; blue for those built between 1850 and 1900, etc. Or you may wish to tie building activity to important dates in your town's history. One color could indicate houses and businesses built before the railroad came through. Another could indicate construction that occurred during the twenty years following that event. You could do the same thing with the date when a large industry moved into town or a superhighway was built.

127

Many people will be interested in the results of your research. And if your display is clear and attractive, you may be able to exhibit it in the public library or other town center.

51

DYNAMIC LANGUAGE

Outage, speechify, publinx, boss, billzapper, rip-off. All these words have appeared recently in newspapers and magazines. Some you might readily identify as slang or new words. Others, like *outage,* have been in the dictionary for at least ten years but have not been frequently used until now. (Outage means electrical power failure.)

Publinx does not appear in dictionaries, but is used by many people to refer to a public golf course (public links). *Boss* now means good or outstanding. In a standard dictionary the word is defined as "a raised ornamentation" or "one who exercises control or authority."

Different interest groups tend to develop a vocabulary all their own. Words like *speed, shoot, trip* belong to the drug culture. People interested in hot cars talk about *patch, stretch, j-ing, drag, draft, cubes, Christmas tree,* etc.

Start a dictionary of terms that are used by particular age and interest groups. It might be centered around a trade, sport, recreation or any activity. Look up the words in a standard dictionary to see if their current usage has any relationship to the dictionary definitions.

Determine how you're going to lay out your dictionary. One approach could be an alphabetical arrangement, with notations about the interest or age group that would ordinarily use the word.

Example:

Words	Standard Usage	Interest Group's Usage
draft	a current of air in a closed space	(racing, automobile) making use of the vacuum created by a leading vehicle so as to maintain speed and conserve fuel by a following vehicle
shoot	to let fly or cause to be driven with force	(drugs) 1. To inject a drug under the skin with a hypodermic needle 2. A gathering of people for the purpose of injecting drugs

Do you think the new words and/or definitions should be included in a standard dictionary? Do you think they add anything to communication? How long do you think a word has to be in use before it is adopted by a standard dictionary?

52

INFLATION SURVEY

The news frequently mentions something called the Consumer Price Index. This index averages the prices of goods (food, clothing, etc.) and services (heat, rent, etc.) bought by the average family. If the index goes up, it means that the average family had to pay more for goods and services. If the index goes down, the average family might have had a little money left over that month.

It might be very instructive and helpful to work up a consumer price index for your family.

Start by making a list of the things your family usually buys. Include food such as milk, bread, eggs, juice, meat, vegetables, etc.; clothes such as shirts, pants, dresses, socks, shoes, etc.; utilities such as oil, gas and electricity; cleaning supplies, toothpaste, books, records, rent and anything else you can think of.

Now make a chart listing these products. Next to the product write in the price. Check your family's bills for the cost of items like electricity, clothing and rent. Go to the store to find out food prices, etc. You might want to compare the prices at several stores. (Who knows? Maybe you can save your family some money.)

After several months, check again to see if the prices your family pays have changed. If the prices on the goods and services in your index have not changed, but your family and the newspapers are still talking about rising prices, check to see where the increase is coming from. You may have left out some important items.

Computing an index like the Consumer Price Index can be difficult. A simplified way is to figure out how much (in percent) the price of each item has changed. For instance, if a carton of milk used to be 30¢ but is now 32¢, the price has increased about 6.6%. Then add all the percent changes together and take the average. The result is your family price index.

A fancier and more complicated way of preparing a family price index (but more revealing) would be to include the fact that your family usually spends more money on milk than on records. So a change in the price of milk will be more important to them than a change in the price of records. If you can't figure out the math for this kind of index, ask your teacher or parents to give you some ideas.

131

53

"ON HOLD" IN MODERN LIFE

Someone once said, "The advantage of traveling on modern highways without stopping for traffic lights has been completely negated by waiting at the toll booths."

And you are probably familiar with a pleasant voice that says: "This is a recording. We are unable to complete your call. Please hang up and dial again. Be sure you are dialing the correct number. This is a recording." In this case the dialer may have made an error. Or the telephone switching station may be overloaded and is simply rejecting the call.

Another example of being "on hold" occurs at gas stations. A driver pulls up to a pump and says, "Fill it up." The attendant sets the automatic pump on "slow" and goes off to wait on another customer.

How much time do we spend "on hold" in modern life? The answer is probably different for every individual and depends a great deal on the kind of job he or she does.

A housewife, who does her shopping early in the morning to avoid the crowds, may find there is only one check-out lane open at that hour. So she ends up waiting in line longer than she might have during peak shopping times.

A salesman has waited seven minutes to see a store manager who is talking on the phone. Finally he's admitted to the manager's office. The phone rings again, and the salesman waits five more minutes until the manager is through with his conversation. How much time does the salesman spend "on hold" during the course of a day or week?

Students also find themselves "on hold." How much time do you spend waiting for school to start when you arrive on the early bus? Waiting after school for the late bus? You are also "on hold" when your teacher has to take time to maintain discipline and when you're dismissed from class or the cafeteria "one row at a time."

In this project, you might try to determine a number of things:

(1) Who has to wait?
(2) What are they waiting for?
(3) How long must they wait?
(4) Who has determined that they should wait?
(5) Does the waiting seem necessary?
(6) Can the waiting be eliminated?
   a) What would have to be done?
   b) How much would it cost?
   c) What effects would it have?

And when you've found the answers to these questions, you might ask if there is a way a person can use his "on hold" time.

54

TAKE A CAN OF CORN

Take a can of corn, a loaf of bread, a jar of pickles or a pound of bologna and trace its history from its beginnings until it is consumed and the package is disposed of.

The goal of this project is to appreciate the work that goes into objects we take for granted. That can of corn, for example, represents the labor of many people.

Of course, a farmer was involved. But who helped the farmer? Where did he get his seed? Who supplied him with his truck, tractor and gasoline to cultivate the field and get the seed planted? When the corn was ripe, who picked it? Was any machinery involved? What happened to the corn then? How was it shucked? Who removed the kernels? How was the corn cooked? Were any spices added? Where did they come from? Who put the cooked corn into cans?

Where did the cans come from? Where was the steel and tin mined? How was it done? Who supplied the fuel and machinery?

After the corn was canned, how were the labels applied? Who designed the labels? Who printed them? How did the labels get to the cannery? How are the labeled cans shipped? In cartons? By train? Who made the cartons? What materials were involved?

Who handles the cans once they are delivered to the store? Who stamps on the prices? Have the cans been inspected? Who handles them at the check-out counter at the supermarket?

The can is home. You open it, eat the corn and throw the can away. What happens to the can now? (See Garbage—Part I for a suggestion for another project.)

You'll probably find that this project takes you all over the world. The label on a can of corn might say that it was packed in Northumberland, Pennsylvania. Locate it on the map. Packing houses are usually located near the source of food, so you can probably assume the corn came from an area within a hundred miles of Northumberland. But what about the tin, steel and paper? Consult an encyclopedia for some of this information. But do as much field research as you can. If you live in an area where food is produced, visit the farm, grain markets, canneries, etc. The key to success in this project is how detailed and accurate your information is.

55

COMMUNITY SURVEY—IS THERE A GENERATION GAP?

The term generation gap is widely used to describe differences of opinion between parents and their children. Experts disagree on the nature of this gap and its effect on such things as family life. What do you think about the generation gap? Is there one in your town?

COMMUNITY SURVEY—IS THERE A GENERATION GAP?

You can start researching this issue by making up a questionnaire. First, write down the questions you think are important. Then write down the answers you are likely to get. Do these answers really tell you anything? Are the answers comparable? Maybe you should give people a choice of possible answers. One way to do this would be to make a statement like, "Most children in this town are well-behaved," followed by a range of answers such as "Agree completely; Agree somewhat; Disagree somewhat; Disagree completely."

Your survey might include a picture of a boy with long hair and a question: "How do you feel about this boy's appearance?" Possible answers: "I like it; I'm neutral; I don't like it." You might also ask questions about current news, both local and national.

Some newspapers publish the questions and results of Gallup and Harris polls. You might use these questions and see if you come up with the same results. Or you might tell your subjects the results of a particular poll and then ask them if they think that poll is an accurate reflection of national opinion. Try to avoid questions that are too personal. "Do you like Mrs. Crebb?" might be embarrassing, particularly if Mrs. Crebb finds out the answers.

When asking questions, try to interview as many different kinds of people as possible. Don't limit yourself to your classmates and their parents, because that won't tell you enough about your town. Find out the ages of the people to whom you speak, but don't write down their names on your sheet. Many people will not answer questions if they have to give their names. You should also explain what you are trying to learn and assure them that you will keep their answers confidential. We suggest that you dress neatly and check to see if there are any local laws to prevent you from conducting this kind of survey.

137

You can use the answers you get in several ways. Compare them by age group: 10–15, 16–20, 21–30, 31–40, and so on. Or you can compare them by occupation as well as age. Do teachers tend to respond more like their students or more like the manager of the grocery store? Can you think of reasons why people respond as they do?

56

ECONOMICS AND YOU

The chances are that 100 years ago if you were sitting around looking at the various items in your home, many of those items would have been made by your family or by one of the shops in your town. Not many would have come from any great distance, and almost none would have come from another country. Much of your food might have been grown in your own garden or on a nearby farm. Your family economy would have been even more local 150 years ago.

Survey the furniture, wall decorations, food and clothing in your home and try to find out where they were made. You can research this in several ways. First, write down the brand names and the names of the stores that sold the goods. Then visit the store and ask the manager, if he's not too busy, where the product was made. If he doesn't know, ask where it was shipped from and write to the shipper. Remember, you can't assume that a product is made in the same place the company has its headquarters. A lot of automobiles are manufactured in Detroit, but many Detroit automobile makers also have factories in other parts of the country.

You can go into more detail if you're willing to write a few letters. Take gasoline, for instance. Did the oil from which the gasoline was made come from Arabia, Texas or Alaska? Where was the gasoline actually manufactured? Where was it stored before it was shipped to your local gasoline station? In the case of hamburger, did the steer come from Argentina, Texas or somewhere else? Where was the animal killed and the meat processed? Chicago and Kansas City used to be the centers for meat processing, but now there are many others.

Regardless of how thoroughly you research this project, you can illustrate your findings on a map. How many products came from another country? How many from another state? Think for a minute about the incredible number of people who have helped to make, ship and sell those products. Think, too, about how widespread is the economy that serves you.

57

CONFORMITY OR INDIVIDUALITY?

To be different is not easy. And being different is not always a good thing. One of the hardest aspects of growing up is learning to think for yourself while conforming enough to relate to friends, enjoy school and live peacefully with your family.

In your school, do your classmates tend to think and act for themselves? Or do they generally follow the crowd—dressing, talking and acting like their classmates? The following experiment can serve as a minor test of the extent to which your classmates are willing to follow the crowd (in this case, you) without really being aware of it.

Your objective is to see how long it takes to introduce a new word. We suggest that the intended meaning be clean and that it be a newly invented word. Some candidates are: grotty, blivit, dorb, snarty, grunk. With the exception of "grotty," a word meaning "lousy," used by British college students, none has any current meaning that we're aware of.

Once you've chosen the word and its meaning, you might start by commenting to a friend, "Man, this day is really blivit." Shake your head as if you're exhausted, roll your eyes and watch his reaction. If your friend thinks for himself, he's liable to say, "Blivit? What does that mean?" Otherwise he'll just go along with you.

140

On the first day, use the word only once (preferably in a group of people) and see if you have any takers. On the second day, use it twice. On the third day, a few more times. If the word doesn't catch on, try a word that sounds a bit more familiar.

To go further in your research, analyze the people who use your word. Are they usually leaders, trend setters in behavior and fashion? Or do they tend to be followers? Are there any differences between the people who first start using your word and those who pick it up later? Does the personality of the first person who adopts your word have any influence on the group's acceptance?

One caution: If you say, "Man, this day is really blivit," and your friend replies, "Yeah, it's really a grunk," drop the whole thing. Your friend has read this book, too.

141

INDEX